Conflict in Urban Transportation

Conflict in Urban Transportation

The People against the Planners

Henry Malcolm Steiner
The George Washington University

Lexington Books
D.C. Heath and Company
Lexington, Massachusetts
Toronto

Library of Congress Cataloging in Publication Data

Steiner, Henry Malcolm.
    Conflict in urban transporation.

    Includes bibliographical references and index.
    1. Urban transportation—Public opinion. 2. Conflict (Psychology)
3. Transportation planning—Citizen participation. I. Title.
HE305.S833   301.5'1   78-2070
ISBN 0-669-02268-3

Published simultaneously in Canada

Printed in the United States of America

International Standard Book Number: 0-669-02268-3

Library of Congress Catalog Card Number: 78-2070

To my students

Contents

List of Figures and Tables

Figures

Tables

Preface

This book is about conflict—the conflict arising between transportation development efforts in cities and the public. The topic is here addressed in two general
sections: the first section of the book focuses on selected case histories and
the second on theoretical matters underlying those histories. In the first section,
the case histories proceed by mode, beginning with cases concerning freeways,
then going on to cases concerning airports, urban rail transport systems, and,
finally, bus mass transit systems. The second part of the book discusses background issues—the philosophical, economic, political, environmental, and social
contexts of the conflict.

In researching these case histories, all of which mostly transpired after the
Second World War, I sensed that a gradual change had taken place in the spirit of
the United States following the war. The nationalism, patriotism, and blind faith
that had prevailed during World War II was slowly disappearing. Many have
pointed to the lack of national unity—that unity so characteristic of the Second
World War—as one of the chief reasons for the erosion of national consensus.
Whatever the cause, there arose a general feeling that the era just past had brought
about the rebirth of individualism, a renascence of respect for the rights of ordinary persons. Postwar affluence in the United States gave people more leisure
to think about the events and constructions that were affecting their lives. Gone
were the days when a national leader could enunciate policy unchallenged. Indeed, people began to question even normal procedures and seemed less willing
in general to accept direction from above. Those who had unquestioningly
obeyed during the war, and their children, found the time and the means to
object—and, in many cases, to object violently. In short, citizens were demand-
ing more community involvement in policy decisions closely affecting their
lives.

The reader may wonder why the cases in this book are taken from the
history of urban transportation and why the theory and background of conflict
are exemplified by cases involving city transport systems. The principal reasons
are that transport systems are ubiquitous, the amounts of money spent on them
have been enormous, and the controversies surrounding them have been highly
publicized. Everyone lives close to some sort of transport facility—street, freeway, railroad, airport. Mobility is a basic necessity. Transport project costs are
measured in millions of dollars, hundreds of millions of dollars, and, in the case
of interstate highways, in tens of billions. All the money spent comes from the
pockets of the populace, and although the path the money takes from pocket
to pocket is not always clear, the fact remains that transportation exacts a heavy
price.

This book could not have been written with the same depth and large number of cases about any field other than transportation. The issue of energy, for

example, has not yet reached the state where it elicits everyone's immediate response as the transport issue does. A book could have been written about pollution, where public response has been strong, but the history of conflict in that area is considerably shorter than in urban transportation. In any case, much of the air pollution is caused directly by our means of transportation—at least in cities.

Finally, I chose cases of confrontation as extreme on the scale of conflict as I could find and, excepting one instance, avoided those conflicts that were solved in an amicable way. Controversy is exciting news because it generates images of crossfire in the minds of readers which the milk-and-water recital of good news does not. I considered the human element in the cases to be most important; while reciting the facts of history, I thought it vital not to forget that the conflicts involved people like ourselves.

Acknowledgments

My first and greatest debt is to the following persons for their invaluable assistance in the preparation of this book: John D. Boggs on the BART case, Spencer M. Eudy on the Los Angeles International Airport case and the political section, Emmett Harrison on the environmental section, Campbell A. Henderson on the Overton Freeway case, James A. Nolen on the BART case, Daniel L. Overbey on the MoPac Expressway case, Judy L. Ramsey on the bus cases, Robert G. Whitener on the social section, and Stephen B. Williams on the philosophical and economic section.

Victoria Arana deserves my unreserved appreciation for her editorial efforts, as does Marian Pierson for so ably directing the typing of a disorderly manuscript.

Many others assisted by providing information on the cases. They have my deep gratitude, although I will not name them since there were so many.

Part I: Cases

1 Parks Are for People

Preserving a park as opposed to allowing an interstate highway to cross it is the basic conflict of this case. For twenty years now, there have been plans for Interstate 40 to bisect Overton Park in Memphis, Tennessee. Interstate 40, which stretches from North Carolina to California, still has a four-mile gap at Memphis, and will have it until the conflict is settled.

The Overton Park case is noteworthy primarily because the courts have been involved. Many tribunals, including the United States Supreme Court, have heard the case and issued rulings.

The background information which follows is not in strict chronological order. Rather than trace the day-by-day history of the case, I have tried to analyze the various elements which have played a role in the controversy.

The Controversy Begins

Few metropolitan areas can boast a forest close to the central business district. Memphis's Overton Park has been called one of the country's finest city forest parks.

The park, consisting of 342 acres, was acquired by the city in 1901. Since then the park has provided its visitors with numerous facilities. Brooks Art Gallery, a bandshell, and formal gardens impart culture to the park's atmosphere. A zoo, well known for breeding rare species, lies on the north edge of the park. At the opposite end, near the south entrance, is a nine-hole golf course. The athletic fields are popular spots within the park. Wading pools abound for the youngsters. A lake and nearby picnic grounds provide a setting for family afternoons. Perhaps the best feature of all is the 170 acres of oak and hickory forest.

Walking down the Overton Park Zoological Trail, one would never guess that downtown Memphis is just a few blocks away. Here, among the trees, the sounds of the surrounding city go unheard. Numerous birds, including some rare migratory species, can be seen. Raccoons, possums, skunks, and an occasional fox also make their homes within the margins of the park. The Secretary of Citizens to Preserve Overton Park, Inc., once commented that she, like so many others, considered the park a part of the city's character and wondered why elected officials would want to destroy it.

The four-mile gap in I-40 is still there. In Memphis, I-40 deadends at I-240. After winding around to the southern part of the city, I-240 connects with I-255, which finally returns to I-40.

In 1953, the city of Memphis began a study to develop a major street plan. In 1955, plans were released for an east-west expressway through Overton Park. Historically, roads follow the paths of least resistance. Harland Bartholomew and Associates, who had the contract for planning this portion of I-40, availed themselves of that time-honored criterion in selecting a route for the highway.

Parks and public lands are chosen as highway sites whenever possible for two reasons. First, since they are public, acquisition costs amount to less. Second, the costs and problems involved in relocating people are avoided. These reductions in immediate costs make a tremendous impact in cost-benefit analyses, which are usually undertaken to show that the route selected is best. The route which was proposed followed a city bus lane through the park. Prior to the bus lane, a railroad trolley had bisected the park. Few thought that a road would be much different.

The road through the park was to be a necessary link in a cross-country interstate system and a vital part of the metropolitan Memphis transportation system as well. The proposed expressway was to provide access to the downtown shopping district. It would take up twenty-six acres of the park and replace the city bus lane. The bus lane, which cut a mere twenty-five-foot swath through the middle of the park, would be replaced by a six-lane corridor, 200 to 250 feet wide, except at the east edge of the park, where a proposed ramp would require about 450 feet. The planners' blueprints were approved at the district level by the Federal Bureau of Public Roads in 1956. The planners then began a series of more detailed studies which lasted into the 1960s.

The Federal Highway Act of 1956 required that a public hearing be held to consider the proposed route. The hearing was held on March 14, 1961. The cost-benefit figures cited to the public were those based on the use of public land. Of course, these figures represented the park route as the least expensive one. The Bureau of Public Roads approved the plans in 1966, but citizen opposition demanded another review. All the same, the route was again approved in 1968.

Meanwhile, the Department of Transportation was established by an act of Congress on October 15, 1966. The Bureau of Public Roads, which formerly had operated in conjunction with the Department of Commerce, was now relocated within the Department of Transportation. Now, not only was a highway corridor hearing necessary, but a highway design hearing was required as well. This hearing was held in May 1969. Despite citizen protests against the park route, the Tennessee Department of Highways recommended approval of the plan to John Volpe, Secretary of Transportation in the Nixon administration.

In 1968, a change occurred in the city government of Memphis. The new council voted its unanimous opposition to the park route for I-40. The action came as a complete surprise to the highway authorities, who immediately scheduled a meeting with the city council. Those present at the meeting were Federal Highway Administrator Lowell K. Birdwell, William S. Pollard, vice-president of Harland Bartholomew and Associates, the firm which had designed the road, Governor Buford Ellington, Tennessee Highway Chief Charles W. Speight, and representatives of the Tennessee Highway Department. The council was told that I-40 would be built through the park or not at all. Realizing the importance of this link, both to state and city, a small majority of the Memphis city council approved the route. The council made an appeal to the new Nixon administration for financial assistance. Volpe temporarily withheld construction funds, but on November 5, 1969, he approved the route. The Tennessee Department of Highways then announced that it would begin taking bids for the construction of I-40 through the park. That action strengthened the determination of the citizens' protest group to prohibit the expressway from transgressing the park's limits.

Public reaction to the highway plans has had a complicated history, too. In July 1956, citizens strongly opposed to the park route held a meeting at Trinity Methodist Church to hear the argument for the park route by a representative from the firm which had made the street plan study. Following that meeting, concerned citizens formed the Committee to Preserve Overton Park. But, for a long time, their attempt to contest the park route made little effective progress.

In 1964, the more powerful Citizens to Preserve Overton Park, Inc., was formed, with Dr. Arlo I. Smith as chairman. In the five years between 1964 and 1969, the group's activities consisted mainly of distributing printed materials and visiting with federal and state officials. However, when the state highway department called for bids for construction through the park, the citizens' organization filed suit in the U.S. District Court in Washington. For the next few years, the courts were to be involved in the controversy.

The Courts Provide a Voice

When Citizens to Preserve Overton Park, Inc., filed suit in the U.S. District Court in Washington, the Sierra Club and the National Audubon Society joined as plaintiffs. On January 23, 1970, the judge ruled that the state highway department must be included in the suit; he therefore referred the case back to the state. He also granted a temporary injunction against construction until March 1.

On February 20, 1970, the case came up for a hearing in the U.S. District Court for the Western District of Tennessee. Nine days later, the judge dismissed the case and awarded judgment to the defendants (the state). The citizen group appealed the case and asked for another temporary injunction, but their request was denied. The group then went to the U.S. Sixth Circuit Court in Cincinnati, Ohio, to get a temporary injunction, which was granted until a hearing could be arranged. A hearing was held on June 15 before three judges who studied the matter until September 29. On that date, the judges voted 2-1 to uphold the lower court's decision, thus dissolving the temporary injunction. A petition was filed for a full hearing in the circuit court. When that was denied, the next body to turn to was the United States Supreme Court.

An application for a stay of action pending a petition for a writ of certiorari (which brings the records of the lower courts to the Supreme Court for review) was filed with the Supreme Court. Justice Potter Stewart granted the stay on November 6, 1970. The other justices supported Justice Stewart, and January 11, 1971, was the date set for the hearing. In the three-page discussion accompanying its decision, the Supreme Court ruled that Congress had not intended to prohibit judicial review of any decision made by the secretary of transportation. At the time Volpe had approved the route, there were no regulations requiring formal, factual findings to accompany the secretary's decision. Now there *was* such a regulation. Nevertheless, the new regulation had not been in effect when the Overton Park route was approved, so the case could not be remanded to the secretary of transportation. Instead, the Supreme Court sent the case back to the U.S. District Court of West Tennessee for a full review of the secretary's approval.

The basis for that decision came from the Transporation Act of 1966, which stated that the secretary of transportation may not authorize the expenditure of federal funds to finance construction of highways through public parks if "prudent and feasible" alternative routes exist. If no alternative route exists, approval can come only if all possible planning has been done to minimize harm to the park. The Supreme Court remanded the Overton Park case to find out if John Volpe had met the two requirements before authorizing federal funding. The lower court was asked by the Supreme Court to make substantial inquiry to see whether the secretary had acted within his authority under the law, and it was told to make sure that the choice itself of a route was not, in the words of Justice Marshall, "arbitrary, capricious, an abuse of discretion, or otherwise not in accordance with the law."

Judge Bailey Brown of the U.S. District Court of West Tennessee heard the case from September 27 to November 4, 1971. The National Wildlife Federation along with three individuals joined with Citizens to Preserve Overton Park, Inc., the Sierra Club, and the National Audubon Society as plaintiffs in the suit. They were represented by law firms from both Memphis and Washington, D.C. The defendants were represented by a host of city, state, and federal attorneys, not to mention private attorneys for the chamber of commerce and the Downtown Association of Memphis. Judge Brown issued his decision in January 1972, sending the case back to Secretary of Transportation John Volpe. Volpe was told to make a route determination according to the procedures set forth in Section 4 of the Transportation Act of 1966.

One of the last things John Volpe did before resigning his position to accept the ambassadorship to Italy was to forbid the use of federal funds for construction of that section of Interstate 40 projected to go through Overton Park. He suggested that the city build a tunnel underneath the park, reroute I-40, or use mass transit. Undaunted, Mayor Wyeth Chandler of Memphis said he would seek state and county money to finance the $18 million expressway through the park.

Secretary of Transportation John Volpe had ruled out the park route, but had not provided an acceptable alternative. Judge Bailey Brown ordered Claude S. Brinegar, Volpe's successor, to establish an alternative route if the park route was deemed imprudent. Brinegar appealed to the U.S. Sixth Circuit Court of Appeals, which overruled Judge Brown. It was not the secretary's responsibility to suggest other prudent and feasible routes.

Alternatives

Because of the controversy surrounding the Overton Park route, many alternative proposals were put forward.

As early as 1958, Harland Bartholomew and Associates proposed two alternative routes as feasible. One was the park route. The other was five blocks north of the proposed park route and used the L & N Railroad right-of-way. The railroad, they suggested, could use the median strip for its tracks, resembling today's Southern Freeway in Memphis.

A medical doctor personally hired an architectural firm to design an alternative route north of the park. His plan called for an elevated road over North Parkway, a present street. The doctor's plan had an unsafe double dogleg in it. The city council vowed it would fight the North Parkway route proposal. When the residents of the area north of the park heard of it, they formed the North Parkway Association to oppose the implementation of any such plans. They feared the destruction of property values and were ready to file suit if necessary.

Another alternative route which was suggested did not have a chance because it would have divided a truly integrated neighborhood, a great source of pride to city officials. City leaders did not want that area disturbed.

One member of the city council proposed a four-lane strip eighty-four feet wide with a concrete divider, instead of the proposed six-lane highway with its forty-foot median strip. The National Safety Council would not accept so few as four lanes through a metropolitan area. Whether or not a four-lane route would have been prudent and reasible was also questioned.

Early in 1975, Tennessee Senator William Brock was considering sponsoring a bill through Congress to get I-40 routed across the park. Since it had taken an act of Congress to authorize construction of the Alaskan Pipeline over the complaints of the environmentalists, many thought that a similarly decisive action was needed to ensure completion of the interstate highway system.

Before Claude S. Brinegar left his position as secretary of transportation in late January 1975, he had narrowed the options for the case down to these three:

1.   cut and cover a tunnel under Overton Park,
2.   route I-40 north of the park, underneath North Parkway, or
3.   do not build at all.

When William T. Coleman, Jr., became secretary of transportation, he ruled out the last two alternatives, stating that there was no prudent and feasible alternative to the route under the park. A cut and cover project under North Parkway would cost $37 million more than a similar project through the park. In addition to greater construction costs, 147 families near North Parkway would have to be displaced, along with eleven businesses. A North Parkway tunnel would have to come dangerously close to two apartment complexes whose inadequate foundations would not withstand tunnel-caused vibration.

Coleman ruled out the no-build alternative as unfeasible because the projected highway was to be part of a nationwide interstate highway system, designed to connect the whole country. Coleman believed the highway necessary to the smooth overall traffic flow of the city and capable of filling a need that mass transit could not meet.

Recent proponents of the park route have pointed to several considerations making it the only feasible one. First, approval has already been given for completing the expressway up to the borders of the park. Second, a new bridge spans the Mississippi River due west of Overton Park, allowing I-40 a straight path through Memphis. And third, the state has already acquired title to the land inside the park for the necessary right-of-way. The $2 million given to the city of Memphis by the state in exchange for this land has already been used by the city to purchase other park land. Responding to what he considered the economic issue, the chief executive officer for Memphis acknowledged that selecting the park route was not an ideal but a pragmatic decision because downtown Memphis would simply continue to be inaccessible otherwise.

For a while, it was thought that Secretary of Transportation William Coleman was leaning toward approving a tunnel bored beneath the park. The tunnel under consideration was to be the widest one in the United States, comparable to the tunnel under the mall of the Capitol in Washington, D.C. Two sixty-five-foot holes would have to be bored side by side to accommodate three lanes each. Besides representing an enormous engineering task, such a tunnel plan would present other problems. In order to prevent seepage, pumps would have to be installed, and these would lower the water table throughout the area. A lower water table would have a definite effect on the vegetation in the park. Lick Creek, which flows through the park, would have to be diverted, probably by the use of a siphon. To pressure the siphon, a reservoir eight feet deep and covering thirty acres would be needed. This much-stagnant water would be an invitation to mosquitoes and malaria. The noise factor would be yet another problem. In 1975 the estimated construction cost of the tunnel was $268.4 million.

On April 21, 1975, Secretary Coleman authorized a $160 million cut and cover construction project through the park, but made it subject to the findings of the required environmental impact statement. The cut and cover method involves cutting a trench, putting the road in, and then covering over the top. What results is a tunnel, except that the ground above it has been disturbed. Coleman approved an eighty-foot trench, but hoped a sixty-foot trench would be all that was necessary. If not, he would approve a width up to 120 feet. His plan to complete the 3.7 mile section of Interstate 40 called for two four-lane roads stacked on top of each other.

Coleman's plan was not without restrictions. No ventilation shafts or other extensions were to protrude above the park surface. The surface was to be restored within one year and replanted to the satisfaction of the Memphis Park Committee by the following year.

Coleman suggested a slurry method of construction, a method new to this country. The procedure is used frequently in Europe, especially in Italy. It involves cutting two narrow trenches and then filling them with slurry, or some other heavy liquid to stabilize the dirt walls. The liquid is then displaced by fluid concrete poured over steel reinforcing rods. Once the concrete has set, excavation can be completed up to each wall to make a trench of the desired width, with no filling necessary. Coleman hoped that by using this method excavation could be limited to a width of sixty feet. The federal government conducted a study to see if the slurry method of construction was possible, given the soil condition of the park, and found that indeed it was.

The estimated $160 million construction cost for such a project allows $100 million for the actual construction and $60 million for landscaping the surface. The city has agreed provisionally to give up the bus right-of-way; thus, with the road going underneath the park, total parkland would increase.

The suggested plan has not been met with enthusiasm by everyone. Opponents point out that it would take fifty to seventy-five years to replace the trees that would have to be cut down. The environmentalists are pre-paring to file another suit saying that Coleman violated federal statutes. Federal statutes require that a route be selected before an appropriate design is determined. They maintain that Coleman did both at the same time.

Opposition is also coming from the state. Tennessee Governor Ray Blanton has said that the state cannot afford its share of the estimated con-struction costs (10 percent of $160 million). The state of Tennessee asserts that the maintenance it must provide on this section would cost between $3.5 and $4 million a year. The governor and the state highway department are holding out for the original depressed road design, estimated in 1975 to cost $26 million.

William S. Pollard of Harland Bartholomew and Associates favors the route through the park because there has been growing support for it in the past sixteen years. Local handouts and maps have long publicized its location. Pollard believes a different plan would only be more disruptive at this time.

The idea for an expressway through Overton Park was proposed twenty years ago. Since then, the proposal has had national news coverage, has spent several years in the courts of our land, including the highest one, has become a hot issue in political races, and has sparked much debate over environmental issues. Those running for mayor of the city of Memphis have always found it necessary to express their feelings about a road through Overton Park.

The federal government, which pays 90 percent of construction costs, favors one plan. The state government is holding out for its own plan. Environmentalists vow to keep the freeway out of the park. Neighboring residential areas are united to keep the road out of their neighborhoods.

Eventually, the courts will have to decide the outcome of the controversy. Arbitrary settlement seems to be the only answer.

Bibliography

Citizens to Preserve Overton Park, Inc., v. Brinegar, U.S. Sixth Circuit Court of Appeals, 794 Federal Reporter, 2nd Series, 1212 (1974).

Citizens to Preserve Overton Park, Inc., v. Volpe, U.S. Supreme Court, 91 S. Ct. 814 (1971)

"Interstate 40 vs. Overton Park," Southern Living, October 1974.

Memphis Commercial Appeal, selected articles.

"Overton Park." Audubon 72 (January 1970): 121.

"Showdown in the Park: Conservationists Action Over Building U.S. Highway Through Overton Park." *Time,* 15 March 1971, p. 44.

"Volpe Retrieves Overton Park." *Audubon* 75 (March 1973): 122.

2 The MoPac Expressway

Austin is the capital of Texas and the home of the University of Texas. Its climate is comfortable and its surroundings pleasant. It is a city without many of the typical urban problems, a happy condition in large part attributable to its economic reliance on clean industries, including governmental and educational concerns. That kind of economic base is relatively free of fluctuations and generally provides steady growth.

One of the urban problems that *does* plague Austin is its traffic—not a bad problem most of the time, but a growing one nonetheless. To handle the constantly increasing traffic load, highways and parking lots are continually being improved and expanded. New highways are being designed and built. As the city grows, so does its traffic, and so must its street and highway network. But one of Austin's new major expressways has run into a caution light, if not a stop sign.

Missouri Pacific Boulevard, MoPac (Missouri Pacific) Expressway, and Loop 1 are all names for the new expressway which, whatever it is called, is guaranteed to generate considerable discussion among any group of Austinites. This chapter briefly explores the controversy's development, dimensions, and possible resolutions.

Historical Development of the Controversy

The concept of a Missouri Pacific Boulevard is over fifty years old. It was first suggested in the 1928 City Plan, which envisioned rerouting the Missouri Pacific Railroad traffic over another line, removing the railroad track, and using the remaining right-of-way for a boulevard. Although the idea of removing the track faded with time, the concept of a boulevard sharing the railroad's right-of-way continued to reappear in subsequent city plans.

Development moved past the planning phase in 1960, when a Street and Bridge Bond Program was approved. The program included funds for street underpasses along the Missouri Pacific Railroad. A year later the city of Austin retained a consultant to begin actual design work for MoPac Boulevard, as the facility was then called. At about the same time the city of Austin reached an agreement with the Missouri Pacific Railroad Company whereby the railroad deeded to the city the outer fifty feet of its right-of-way on each side of the tracks between Hancock Drive and West 5th Street. In return, the city agreed

11

to eliminate all grade-level street crossings within those limits. The city received the right-of-way needed for the long-planned MoPac Boulevard, and the railroad was relieved of responsibility for numerous street crossings in the west Austin neighborhoods.

By 1961 MoPac Boulevard was firmly established as part of the Austin planning scene. It was included in numerous city transportation plans developed during the 1960s. The most important plan was the *Austin Transportation Plan 1962-1982,* created by the city of Austin, Travis County, and the Texas Highway Department under the auspices of the federal Bureau of Public Roads. In that plan, the concept of MoPac Boulevard was changed from a four-lane limited access highway to a full-fledged expressway. The idea for the MoPac Expressway was born.

The *Austin Transportation Plan 1962-1982* was a result of the 1962 Federal Highway Act, which required cities with populations of over 50,000 to develop and continuously update a master transportation plan. The Federal Highway Act set forth specific procedures to be followed in the development and revision of these plans, including the participation of various levels of government. In order to qualify for federal aid, highway projects within the urban area would have to conform to this master plan.

When MoPac Boulevard was redesigned as an expressway in the *Austin Transportation Plan,* it was given the highest priority for construction. The plan was important for yet another reason: it conveyed much of the spirit and philosophy prevalent in highway planning at that time. Most noticeable was the heavy emphasis on strictly technical factors related to the engineering design of various street facilities, and the consequent de-emphasis on the integration of those facilities with the areas to be served. The plan outlined in detail how travel time saved could be regarded as a major benefit of the project. Regarding land use, it stated that the proposed expressways were located to serve the areas connected and would not cause adverse changes in land use.

In light of later developments, it is noteworthy that, at the time the report was made, the area to be traversed by MoPac was recognized to be primarily residential, although some public, park, and recreational land would be crossed also. Maps projecting future land usage anticipated no substantial changes.

The plan relied heavily on standards set by the National Committee on Urban Transportation (NCUT) in determining the degree of need for local facilities. By 1964, the city was to have 10.4 miles of expressway (Interstate 35), or 1.4 percent of the total street mileage. NCUT suggested it be 2 to 5 percent. On the basis of NCUT recommendations, the plan called for a total of 56.2 miles of expressway to be built and in operation by 1982. As is often the case, a number of the expressways planned were obsolete before serious planning could begin. The MoPac Boulevard Expressway, which had been planned for some time, was further along in development and was indicated as the most needed of all the expressways recommended.

Inclusion of MoPac Expressway in the *Austin Transportation Plan* cleared the way for further action. The city had most of the right-of-way, a preliminary plan, and funding for some grade-separation projects. One element was missing. A project the size of MoPac would require resources beyond those of the city of Austin. In 1966, city officials and officials of Travis County met with the Texas Highway Commission to request the assistance and financial participation of the Texas Highway Department in the development of a controlled-access highway along the route identified as Missouri Pacific Boulevard. The commission agreed to participate and the route was established from F.M. Road 1325 south to U.S. Highway 290.

A joint agreement was signed by the Austin City Council, Travis County Commissioners Court, and the Texas Highway Department specifying the duties of each party. In essence, the city would acquire right-of-way in the city and provide for utility relocation services; the county would provide half the right-of-way outside the city; and the state would provide the other half of the right-of-way outside the city and would supervise the construction. The expressway to be designated as a state highway, Loop 1.

Events now began to move quickly. After the 1966 agreement was signed, the Texas Highway Department began detailed planning work, and in December 1967 submitted a schematic layout to the Bureau of Public Roads. One month later the department submitted a route-sketch map to the bureau. A public hearing was set for February 1968.

At the public hearing on February 6, a schematic of the proposed facility was shown. As stated in the *Special Report on the MoPac Expressway*, "No objections concerning the route were received." It was also noted that "due to very extensive discussions and meetings prior to the public hearing, very little comment was received on the design features of the facility."

Similar reports appeared in the *Austin American Statesman*. The 500 people in attendance were said generally to approve the plan. The hearing was reported as the last public formality before the Texas Highway Department could enter the construction phase of the MoPac project. Approvals by the Regional Planning Commission and the federal Bureau of Public Roads were now all that remained to be acquired.

But there had been some criticism at the hearing, primarily over the amount of traffic that would be carried on First Street. Concern was also expressed over one-way access roads and about the increased east-west traffic through residential areas. A west Austin neighborhood group had requested a closed meeting with the city council to discuss a bond issue for east-west thoroughfares, but at the February hearing it supported MoPac wholeheartedly. One local engineer noted that the connecting streets might prove insufficient for the increased traffic load between MoPac and the downtown university areas. In general, however, the project was approved. The state representative commited that the expressway would be noisy, intrusive on personal property, and costly in terms of personal income lost, but he remarked that so far he had not seen a better solution of the city's traffic problems.

After the hearing, the Regional Planning Commission held a special meeting at the Highway Department District Headquarters and took only ten minutes to approve plans for the six-lane expressway.

One year after the public hearing, in February 1969, the first part of the MoPac Expressway project was contracted. The project's phases were outlined as shown in table 2-1.

Controversy Catches MoPac

During the early 1970s construction pushed forward. It appeared the first part of phase one would be completed on schedule, allowing the Northland Drive-Bee Caves Road section to be in operation by the autumn of 1975. But as MoPac was quickly becoming a reality, many residents in nearby neighborhoods began having second thoughts. Some citizens opposed the project entirely after seeing it on the ground, but they were a small minority.

A much larger group was concerned over the east-west traffic that would flow through neighborhood streets. An informal coalition of various neighborhood groups, this large group actively called, in early 1975, for the closing of certain interchanges. Originally the coalition suggested that the Westover Road, Windsor Road, and Enfield Road ramps be removed. The *Special Report on the MoPac Expressway*, prepared by the city of Austin and the Texas Highway Department in April 1975, stated that the three interchanges (the ramps in question) were 75 to 90 percent completed and that it was too late to consider their removal. Furthermore, the work was already under contract; there was no time to alter or redesign. The report noted that the designs were similar to those of the 1961 Cotton Report (the preliminary design) and had been a matter of public record since that time. A heavy investment had already been made in the ramps (see table 2-2). The report stated that unilateral action by the city of Austin to alter or close any ramp or portion of the facility would constitute a breach of contract and place the entire project in jeopardy. In addition, since all ramps were constructed legally, after public hearings and previous approval by the Austin City Council, Texas Highway Department, and the Federal Highway Administration, alterations in the ramps could only be made if based on an engineering study and subject to the subsequent appropriate approval by all the agencies involved. It was determined that the Texas Highway Department and the city of Austin could implement ramp alterations only to remove design deficiencies reported in the engineering study—but would have to do so after joint agreement. While other aspects of the *Special Report* became subjects of controversy, its findings concerning ramp removal have been proven truthful and prophetic.

Table 2-1
MoPac Expressway Construction Schedule

Construction	Contract Date	Completion Date
Phase One		
R.M. 2222 and MP RR in Austin	February 1969	July 1970
Northland Drive, 45th Street, and 35th Street Overpasses	December 1969	November 1972
Westover Road, Windsor Road, and Enfield Road Overpasses	March 1970	October 1971
North Bank of Colorado River south to R.M. 2244	February 1971	June 1973
North of Northland Drive (R.M. 2222) south to Enfield Road	July 1972	August 1975 (estimated)
Town Lake Interchange 1st, 5th and 6th Streets[a]	March 1972	August 1975 (estimated)
Main Line Ramps at Town Lake Interchange	b	
Northland Drive north to U.S. 183	b	
U.S. 183 Interchange	b	
Phase Two		
Northern extension from U.S. 183 to F.M. 1325 (Burnet Road)		
Southern extension from Bee Caves Road to U.S. 290 West		

[a] After completion of the first six projects in Phase One, MoPac would be opened from Northland Drive south to Bee Caves Road.

[b] Dates for these projects are not yet scheduled.

One of the highly contested parts of the report was an analysis, done by the Planning and Research Division of the Texas Highway Department, of the ramps' effect on traffic flows. Using actual 1972 traffic-flow volumes, the study found that only three streets would have volume increases over 20 percent: First Street (57 percent), Fifth Street (31 percent), and Westover Road (23 percent). Each of these were east-west streets; none would be over what

Table 2-2
Investment in Westover, Windsor, and Enfield Interchange Ramps

| | Direct Expenditures | | | Net Additional Acquisitions | |
Location	City	State	Total	Houses	Land Parcels
Westover	$ 365,000	224,000	589,000	9	10
Windsor	669,000	403,000	1,072,000	21	17
Enfield	369,000	2,441,000	2,810,000	34	5
Totals	$1,403,000	3,068,000	4,471,000	64	32

road engineers designate as its "street restraint volume," or capacity. On the other hand, nine streets would have decreases of more than 20 percent. Eight of the nine were north-south streets paralleling MoPac, and their projected decreases were rated between 22 percent and 71 percent.

Responding to the suggestion that Westover, Windsor, and Enfield ramps be closed, the analysis indicated that only Westover could be closed (according to 1972 figures) without causing other nearby feeder streets to exceed capacity. The recommendations made by the city were:

1. that ramps be opened upon completion of MoPac,
2. that special controls be installed for ramps at the Westover, Windsor, and Enfield interchanges, and
3. that special ramp control study be authorized to monitor traffic patterns and develop transportation and land-use strategies to protect neighborhoods streets, maintain acceptable traffic levels on arterial streets, and maximize mobility and safety.

The *Special Report's* recommendations were the subject of a hearing held by the city on June 12, 1975, in the Municipal Auditorium and reported in the *Austin American Statesman.* Over 4,000 public notices were mailed to property owners in west Austin for what may have been the largest hearing in city history. Consulting engineer June Melton, speaking for neighborhood groups, said the city's figures in the report predicted massive traffic problems in five years on the east-west feeders. A report on the Ninth and Tenth Street Improvements Project, conducted by a consulting firm under city authorization, indicated MoPac traffic to the city core would quickly cause congestion. Assistant City Manager Homer Reed, however, cited the city report's indication that the neighborhoods involved would have much less traffic with the ramps open.

Reed noted that MoPac's limited access, the special feature of this traffic artery, would separate it from the neighborhood and preserve the community.

Neighborhood groups saw it differently. As their own report indicated, those who conceived MoPac thirty years ago and drew up plans fifteen years later were not concerned about the preservation of neighborhoods. The neighborhood groups pointed out that, in fact, routing often was consciously made through older areas in hopes that redevelopment would ensue.

Like so many similar hearings in highway controversies elsewhere, the June 1975 hearings produced more heat than light. Indeed, the only enlightening point may have been City Manager Dan Davidson's observation that the city could only recommend that the state highway department close the ramps.

One criticism leveled at the *Special Report's* analysis was its use of 1972 traffic volume data. A spokesman for the neighborhood groups termed the procedure absurd, since MoPac was not built in 1972. He suggested that the study did not use projected figures because, had they done so, the study would show just how quickly neighborhood streets would become overcrowded. Also, the report assumed only the Bee Caves-U.S. 183 segment as open, which entirely left out of consideration additional traffic from Phase II extensions. The *Special Report* stated (on page 19) that 1972 actual figures were used because traffic volumes projected for 1990 would be fanciful. The report estimated, using the 1972 figures as a base, that by 1980 traffic volume on residential/collector streets would increase less than 10 percent and less than 20 percent on arterial streets. Whatever the case, it appears the *Special Report* figures were designed to be quite conservative in estimating future traffic levels.

By September 1975, MoPac was a regular topic in the press and at city council meetings. Representing the neighborhood coalition, lawyer Anna Drayer termed MoPac a threat to Austin. She recommended that MoPac be redesigned as a limited-capacity system, citing enormous noise and air-pollution problems if it were not redesigned. The coalition's objective was to ensure that those portions of MoPac not yet completed be replanned to operate as a limited-capacity system. The condition hoped the expressway would serve the existing neighborhoods of the West Austin Corridor without ruining the quality of life in them. Former U.S. Senator Ralph Yarbrough opposed the phase two extensions because they would mean admitting truck traffic into the neighborhoods.

A number of the worries of west Austin groups were well founded. The middle section of MoPac (that which was already built or under construction) was designed before the federal Environmental Protection Act came into effect. Representatives of the citizens' group have stated that expressway noise levels would render 100 to 150 houses ineligible for financing under Federal Housing Administration or Veterans' Administration mortgages due to noise levels exceeding Housing and Urban Development Department standards.

Professor John Gallery (of the Community and Regional Planning School, University of Texas) headed one neighborhood group opposing certain aspects of MoPac. Professor Gallery noted that some residences were within fifty feet of frontage roads, and that MoPac would fail to qualify under their then-current

EPA standards on several counts. Gallery recommended that the phase two extensions be deleted, the Westover-Windsor-Enfield ramps be closed, and MoPac be used strictly as a city facility.

Austin realtor Thurman Blackburn took the opposing view. As reported in the *Daily Texan*, he publicly urged the city to finish right-of-way acquisition and complete MoPac to U.S. 183 (Phase I). He claimed that completion would strengthen the integrity of neighborhoods by taking traffic off neighborhood streets and putting it on a state-maintained facility. Blackburn observed that the savings in street maintenance could be used to pave streets never before paved. As a "Gateway to Austin," Blackburn said, MoPac could be a model thoroughfare. Landscaping, sound barriers, and billboard-prohibition laws would achieve that goal.

That southern extension of MoPac came into a controversy of its own during October 1975. State Senator Lloyd Doggett charged that state highway officials had backdated "firm offer" letters to acquire land between Loop 360 and U.S. 290, despite a Federal Highway Administration directive not to do so. The FHA had forbidden land acquisition negotiations for that section in a letter dated January 5. According to local newspaper accounts, the MoPac southern extension project was one of eighty-three federally funded projects throughout the state which were to be halted because a federally approved environmental impact statement had not been made. Two former state highway department appraisers signed affidavits accusing a right-of-way engineer with backdating letters to evade the FHA restriction. Several parcels were quickly bought by the county at prices above those recommended by state appraisers. (Remember that under the 1966 agreement the state and county each provided half of the right-of-way outside the city. The state assisted the county by providing appraisals and performing other related functions.)

Senator Doggett charged that these purchases were made so MoPac land acquisition would be closer to completion, thereby allowing less time for fruitful opposition from citizens and the Austin Transportation Study. The ATS, which was working on a new Austin Transportation Plan to update the 1962 plan (as required by federal highway laws), could not say whether the southern extension would be included in the new plan or not, and if it were, whether it would be a boulevard or an expressway. The outcome would determine just how much land the southern extension requires. Even so, there is disagreement as to whether the ATS can change MoPac or not. Some sources feel that the 1966 contract precludes any ATS action.

The county commissioner's court had routinely approved the purchases for MoPac, but, according to the county commissioner, all future right-of-way expenditures would be closely scrutinized before approval. He admitted that when it became apparent federal funds would be halted because an environmental impact statement had not been filed, his office had no notion of the authority of the ATS.

Assistant County Attorney Phil Lerway told the *Daily Texan* he saw nothing illegal about the way the land was being acquired but he wondered all the same why the highway department was speeding up the land acquisition. Texas Highway Department Chief Right-of-Way Engineer L.E. Clarke said that the right-of-way engineer involved may indeed have hurried the letters, but that it was not immoral to do so.

While the county was looking into its land purchases, opponents were still arguing the fate of the three interchanges before the Austin City Council. This council, more liberal than earlier ones, found itself restricted by the 1966 agreement. State District Highway Engineer Travis Long said the department would not help finance the study, but would not prohibit the city from closing the ramps for short periods of time as part of the study. Some members of the city council, however, wanted the ramps to remain closed when the expressway was opened by the state on November 1, 1975, and they wanted the ramps to stay closed except for short study periods. Since the consultants could not draw up a schedule for their study until after MoPac was opened, it was doubtful that the city could keep the ramps closed.

In the spring of 1975, the council voted to close the Westover interchange ramps. In response, Texas Highway Department District Engineer Travis Long sent a letter to the mayor stating that ramp construction had progressed too far to be abandoned precipitously, but that the department would honor the city's request and build permanent guard rails across the ramps. The guard rails never came to pass. In a letter dated October 7, Long informed the city that all ramps would be operative when the expressway opened on November 1. Access control, he reminded the mayor, is a legal prerogative of the state, and Long believed the facility would work best with the ramps open.

Austin Mayor Jeff Friedman was angered by the highway department's sudden change of attitude. Friedman was asked if the lack of definite agreement on the ramps question was embarrassing. He replied that he had thought the department would work with the city. He made it clear that he could not be embarrassed by the highway department's saying one thing and doing another. The argument grew more heated and personal when Travis long was described by Friedman as "two-faced" on a local television news program. Meanwhile, highway department officials at the district office were under orders not to comment on the situation. The assistant district engineer had previously told a reporter that the state was really not involved in the controversy; it was only building the highway under a contract from the city. Soon thereafter even District Engineer Long was refusing to comment, preferring to wait until after the upcoming city council meeting.

Certain city council members recommended caution in any action that might be taken, lest state highway aid on other projects be jeopardized. Deputy City Manager Homer Reed said the city would be asking for trouble if it closed ramps unilaterally. The results of the consultant's study could be used to

convince the state and federal groups involved to close permanently, change,
or move the ramps. Were the city to close the ramps without the sanction of a
study, it might be held liable for repayment of all state and federal aid on the
project. Nevertheless, Reed supposed that if the council were to take action
unilaterally in violation of its agreement with the state, then the staff would
surely implement the council's decision.

The city's legal department found that control over the ramps had been
clearly established with the state highway commission, in a memorandum
dated October 21, 1975. The memorandum stated that agreements to assume
another's responsibility have generally been constituted by the courts to go
against public policy and accordingly were not to be recommended. Mayor
Friedman, himself an attorney, agreed that the state could not transfer its
responsibility (that is, its share of costs) to the city in this manner.

Before the legal questions arose, Mayor Friedman had also reached agreement with the highway department on two other matters: to implement council
resolutions banning heavy truck traffic and to set a 45 mph speed limit on the
expressway. However, the Texas Highway Department's change of heart regarding the ramp closings was followed by other unexpected changes.

On November 1, 1975, MoPac Expressway (State Loop 1) was inaugurated
as planned—with all ramps open. The city council had considered a motion to
place its own barricades at the interchanges, but the motion had failed. City
officials believed such an action would have been illegal under both the 1966
contract and state law. Numerous west Austin citizens were outraged at the
council's decision, even though many council members voting against the motion did so reluctantly and said so.

In short, the expressway was opened without ceremony. Highway department crews removed the barricades and the new expressway was off to a poor
start. The legal speed limit was 55 mph, but no speed limit signs were installed.
Joe Ternus, director of the Urban Transportation Department, explained that
the signs were deleted in the hopes that motorists would drive more slowly.
Installing the 55 mph signs would have strained public relations by rubbing salt
in the wounds of the west Austin neighborhood groups.

Proposals for the lower 45 mph speed limit and for closing certain ramps
were to be studied by the city's consultants. The Texas Highway Department
agreed to give the consultants authority over these aspects of traffic control for
brief study periods. Before any permanent changes could be made, though,
the Texas Highway Department and the Federal Highway Administration would
have to grant approval.

MoPac—the Look Back, the Look Ahead

It is perhaps all too easy, watching a hot controversy like this one, to want to
keep score, observe the contest, and root for a side. Less exciting, but definitely

more important to an understanding of the situation, is the analysis of what caused the antagonism in the first place and what allowed it to grow. It is simply not a case of the cranks set against the cookbook engineers. Nor is it possible to declare with impunity that one or the other side is right. Valid arguments are too numerous on both—or all—sides.

There are more plausible explanations. Public opinion has changed rapidly during the last decade and has left the governmental bureaucracy behind, seemingly stalled by institutional inertia. Because of the extremely long lead time required to plan and build a project such as MoPac, bureaucratic inertia might *appear* to be the cause of the problem, even if it were not. If the minimum lead time for a project were ten years, and if the highway department were to change its procedures on all new projects exactly when public attitudes change, the actual physical changes would not be seen until at least ten years later. This, of course, assumes an immediate response by the public agency to changes in public opinion, which obviously cannot always be the case.

Mr. Max Ulrich of the Austin Transportation Study explained that the inertia is not always a product of the bureaucracy itself. The Austin Transportation Study, Texas Highway Department, and almost all other government agencies operate on a budget set by elected officials. These budgets are established for one or two years and govern the functions to be performed by each agency. Little if any funds are allowed for activities not covered by the budget. Together with other laws and rules of procedure, agency activities are specifically outlined.

The use of environmental impact statements, for example, might at first appear to be a symptom of bureaucratic inertia. The Texas Highway Department's procedures, as we know, did not include provision for such statements. Neither did its budgets; apparently the Texas legislature saw no need for such statements either. The highway department pushed its budget to the limits to give the state a very good highway system—even critics agree to this. However, when the ecology movement of the 1960s led to passage of the Environmental Protection Act, and when federal highway aid was tied to environmental considerations (specifically by requiring an impact statement), the department was given the direction and incentive to follow stricter ecological standards.

The division of responsibility among assorted agencies has often compounded problems. While such a division is essential to good organizational functioning, it has too often been cited as a reason for lack of cooperation and coordination. The 1962 *Austin Transportation Plan* indicated little concern for land-use changes. From the strictly technical standpoint of its authors, a transportation plan need not be concerned with land-use changes. From a technical perspective, the only way land use could change would be for a zoning change to occur, and zoning changes are the domain not of transport agencies but of the zoning board. Of course, there is no getting around the fact that an expressway causes changes to be made—at least indirectly. By coordinating all aspects of the land-use problem in the initial planning, conflicts between agencies and their objectives could at least be minimized. For MoPac and other projects begun before the Environmental Protection Act, citizens were forced to rely solely on zoning ordinances in their opposition to commercialization and other land-use changes.

The creation of the Austin Transportation Study was also the outcome of conflict among sources of governmental authority. The 1962 Federal Highway Act required cities of populations over 50,000 to coordinate transportation planning at all government levels and to formulate master transportation plans for their entire area. Previously, each government entity went its own way, participating in joint efforts only on certain individual projects. Each agency also had its own hearing procedures for public involvement. Citizen input was often sparse because of the multitude of processes involved, and because most planning went on within the confines of the agency. Hearings often were unveilings of the finished product instead of working sessions. State highway projects were required to have only one route hearing and one design hearing. These could be combined into one hearing (as MoPac's was), and planners were under no obligation to act on any of the recommendations presented.

The 1962 Environmental Protection Act and subsequent amendments have replaced the simple route hearing with the required master transportation plan, at least for urban areas. The route for any proposed facility must be consistent with the plan, or the study group can veto federal funding for the project. Instead of reducing public input, as one might expect from a procedure which lays its plans out in advance, the new method greatly increases public involvement. Currently the 1962 plan is undergoing a complete revision. The comprehensive review began with the Austin Tomorrow goals program, and involved a lengthy series of hearings in 1974. The Transportation Study met with over twenty-six neighborhood groups just to formulate its new plan and, before presenting the plan for a final hearing early in 1976, intended to convene still more meetings. Even after approval, the plan would be subject to constant scrutiny and revision.

The motive for establishing the Austin Transportation Study, setting it apart from all local governments and giving it veto power over federally funded projects, was to insure that conflicting interests be impartially considered and properly balanced in the making of transportation decisions. The study group sought input from individuals, local groups, and its standing committees of local government officials. Its policy advisory committee consisted of a number of elected officials from the city of Austin and from Travis County, five state legislators, and the district's representative in Congress, J. J. Pickle. Its steering committee consisted of members of the policy advisory committee and administrative professionals working at the city, county, and state levels. The committees provided feedback to both the study group and the governments involved.

By 1975 the study group was in a unique position to balance the needs of potentially affected local neighborhoods and those more widely dispersed groups needing transportation facilities through the local area. Its nonallegiance to any specific government now allows it to serve all potentially affected citizens. The study group is also in a better position than the government agencies to weigh the relative advantages of various transport modes because governmental agencies are often dedicated to a single mode. Even so, to be credible and viable, the study must have massive public input; otherwise governmental bodies can render it ineffective. There is hope that the massive doses of continuing public involvement can prevent or greatly diminish possible recurrences in the future of such controversies as have surrounded MoPac.

Much of the work on MoPac was done before the new procedural changes took effect. Resolution of the conflicts generated by MoPac construction will come, eventually, but it will have to be through established channels, either through the various elected bodies or the courts. Regardless of its final outcome, the MoPac case should cause all concerned citizens to examine closely the adequacy of existing planning and decision-making procedures.

Bibliography

Austin American Statesman. Austin, Texas (various issues).
Austin Transportation Plan, 1962-1982. City of Austin, Travis County, and Texas Highway Department. Austin, Texas, 1965.
The Daily Texan. University of Texas, Austin, Texas (various issues).
Johnson, Bill M. "City Planning History on MoPac." Interoffice memorandum to Mr. T.K. Wood, January 26, 1968 (furnished by Max Ulrich).
Special Report on the MoPac Expressway. City of Austin and Texas Highway Department. Austin, Texas, 1975.

3 Los Angeles International Airport

The Los Angeles International Airport case illustrates the sort of conflict that has developed between the public and the air transport mode. The fact that the airport is located in Los Angeles is not important. It might have been any major airport near any large urban community. Los Angeles International Airport—or LAX, as it is commonly abbreviated in the three-letter International Civil Aviation Organization airport code—provides a good example because the development of conflict has advanced to the final stages. That is, the courts have entered the conflict to rectify an injustice and, in at least one suit, all legal avenues have been exhausted including an appeal to the Supreme Court. The LAX case also illustrates the dilemma in which a city or county administration may find itself when attempting to find a solution acceptable to both the public and the aviation industry.

Los Angeles is a city of people—three million people—all coming and going, moving by cars, buses, ships, trains, and airplanes. That is how Los Angeles appears to a casual visitor caught in the freeway rush or the airport crowds. Despite the first impression it makes, Los Angeles has an appeal that draws people from all over the world; some come just to visit, some to stay. It is a sprawling metropolis composed of a cluster of urban communities separated merely by white signs to inform travelers when they have passed from one into another. It is served by the Sante Fe, Union Pacific, Southern Pacific, and Amtrak railroads, six major bus lines, and thirty-six domestic and international airlines. Great numbers of airplanes seem to be landing or taking off continually from LAX—or so it seems to those who live near it.

In 1973, Los Angeles International Airport, the world's third-busiest airport, handled 491,121 landings and takeoffs, 23,501,697 passengers, and 1.3 billion pounds of air cargo. The airport, covering more than 3,000 acres, sprawls like the city. It has six major terminals designed to handle simultaneously ten jet aircraft, each carrying 150 passengers. Of course, all of this activity cannot take place without problems. It is significant that, in the past five years, LAX's major difficulties have not been operational, but relational. The airport has been unable to maintain harmonious relations with the communities adjoining the airport. This is the story of the airport's growth and its growing pains.

The Los Angeles area has long been a center of aviation activity. The first transcontinental flight, by Galbraith Rodgers, landed at nearby Pasadena on November 5, 1911, and the first round-the-world flight took off from Santa

Monica on March 17, 1924. Only three years ofter that signal event, a committee
selected the site for what is now the Los Angeles International Airport. An area
of approximately 640 acres located near the Pacific Ocean was chosen so that
planes landing and taking off could take advantage of the prevailing east-west
winds. The site was fifteen miles southwest of downtown Los Angeles in an
area no one anticipated would interfere with the city's growth. In 1927, there
were only two incorporated communities within five miles of the site, Inglewood
and El Segundo. Far from the population centers of those communities, the
airport site did not appear to be detrimental to either.

Mines Field, as LAX was originally named, was completed in 1928. It had a
2,000-foot, oiled-dirt runway and a terminal building. These facilities were
built with local financing because the federal government had specifically pro-
hibited aid for airports in the Air Commerce Act of 1926. However, under that
act, the secretary of commerce was authorized to establish, operate, and maintain civil airways, a provision which opened the door for governmental promotion of civil aviation.

Between 1929 and 1939, Mines Field, except for the fact that it would one
day become the Los Angeles International Airport, played a minor role in the
chain of events that would one day cost Los Angeles millions of dollars; its
future was being shaped elsewhere in the United States and the world.

October 29, 1929, marked the beginning of a severe financial crisis which
would affect the world for more than a decade. Los Angeles, although less
affected than other parts of the United States, became more concerned with
recovering from the Panic of 1929 and the ensuing depression than with aviation
as such. However, it soon became apparent that aviation would certainly con-
tribute a fair share to the area's economic recovery.

By 1926, aviation technology had advanced independently to the stage
where government regulation and promotion were economically feasible. The
Air Commerce Act was promulgated that year. It encouraged development of
civil aviation, but its administration was divided among several government
agencies. The success achieved under its provisions was, consequently, less than
optimal. The civil air industry needed more than governmental promotion to
develop—it needed capital.

The Panic of 1929 dried up most large sources of development capital. Few
investors had the foresight to invest in a fledgling aviation industry. The lack
of capital limited large-scale industrial growth and resulted in the development
instead of several small aircraft and aircraft parts manufacturers, which per-
force were undercapitalized. The same stringent conditions prevailed for commercial air carriers. There were fourteen domestic lines in 1929; most were
concerned with carrying airmail and not passengers. An airmail contract from
the government ensured a steady income, even if the carrier had not bid high
enough to cover its out-of-pocket costs. Underbidding often resulted in the

failure of a carrier and served to underline the insecurity and instability of the industry. Investors became increasingly skeptical of the industry's future.

Nonetheless, the depression years were also distinguished by a number of significant events in aviation. Between 1930 and 1939, the transcontinental nonstop flight time was reduced substantially: in 1930 Roscoe Turner flew from New York to Los Angeles in 18 hours and 43 minutes and Howard Hawkes flew from Los Angeles to New York in 12 hours and 25 minutes. In 1937, Howard Hughes flew from Burbank, California, to Newark, New Jersey, in 7 hours and 28 minutes. These individual efforts had more psychological impact on the American public at that time than they would have had in normally prosperous times. The public could not help getting caught up in the enthusiastic acclamation of feats which tended to romanticize aviation, since individual achievements rather than industrial accomplishments were applauded.

During the 1930s, Pan American Airways carried the American flag to every continent in the world and, quite independently, was becoming the world's largest international carrier. With its subsidiaries, Pan American was covering 87,000 route miles connecting forty-seven countries.

During this period, California was not as depressed economically as other parts of the country. A segment of the population from the depressed Midwest and Southwest began moving to California in hopes of finding employment. Because of its diverse economic base, the Los Angeles area attracted a disproportionately large share of this new labor force. It also attracted several aircraft manufacturers.

Six thousand miles away from Los Angeles, in Germany, aeronautical technology was also advancing. Like most of the industrial nations, Germany was developing its civil air transportation capability. At the end of World War I, Germany had been stripped of its air arms, along with its other capabilities to conduct offensive warfare. However, Germany had been developing its civil aviation in such a way that rapid conversion to military uses was possible. Pilot training programs were being conducted under the guise of sport gliding activities. Thus did Germany procure a large number of semiqualified pilots.

In the Far East, Japan's military leaders were openly developing military aviation as rapidly as possible to support Japan's invasions of the Asian mainland and the Southwest Pacific. The world was on the brink of war, and all that was needed to start it was a hostile incident. Germany supplied it in September 1939 with a surprise attack on Poland. President Roosevelt and the American leaders proclaimed in response that the American industrial base would be used to aid the cause of freedom.

The start of the war in Europe initiated the first big step toward the development of an aerospace industry in the Los Angeles area. Los Angeles already had several aircraft manufacturers who needed only capital to expand. In

addition, there was an abundance of under-employed laborers who had moved
to California from the depressed areas. The contracts let to California aviation
enterprises by the federal government in 1939 and 1940 were all that was
necessary to start a period of economic expansion in the local aviation industry.

This brief account of a few events occurring between the construction of
Mines Field in 1928 and the start of World War II may not appear to be ger-
mane to the story of the Los Angeles International Airport and its problems
in the 1970s. But consider what really happened in those years. Los Angeles
constructed an airport which at the time appeared to be well out of the
growth vectors of the Los Angeles communities. The industry which this
airfield was to serve was given a relatively free hand in developing along the
strongest technological lines. There was free entry into the industry because of
low capitalization. Anyone who discovered an engineering innovation that
might possibly improve aircraft performance could enter the market with a
patent and a garage workshop. By 1938, when Congress began to amend the
Air Commerce Act of 1926, the imminence of war in Europe and Asia demanded
that the government promote and accelerate the aeronautical industry's development. Little thought was given to the impact of new technology on the physical
and social environment. It cannot be denied that in academic circles the impact
was being debated, but existing academic theories were simply and understandably not being applied to monitor the growth of this vital industry. When the
advent of the new aviation technology is considered in the context of the
troubled economy of the 1930s, one can appreciate a general reluctance to
apply any controls which might detract from welcome economic benefits. When
the events of the 1930s are viewed historically, it is easy to see the development
of serious, if latent, problems.

If Southern California and the Los Angeles area had already attracted a
large number of people from the depressed areas, the rapid expansion of the
aeronautical industry and start-up of other defense-related industries only further
encouraged an abnormal population growth, with its concomitant rapid development of the metropolis and surrounding communities.

Mines Field became the site of two aircraft manufacturers, and soon the
traffic in and out of the field reached a record level. Because of the ever-increas-
ing demand for housing, the communities around the airport began to creep
closer and closer to the boundaries of the field. Certainly there were some complaints over the increased noise generated by the activities at the field; however,
everyone recognized that the nation was at war and everyone had to endure
some of the hardships. Therefore, the majority, if not all, of the complaints
were smothered under the blanket of patriotism.

By 1944, United States production of war planes reached a record level,
with a total of 97,649 planes produced that year alone. The following year
there was a sharp decline in the production of combat aircraft, but by December
1945, American manufacturers had orders for more than 40,000 planes for use

as civil air transports. It was a simple matter to shift production. That very year, international commercial service to both Europe and the Far East was resumed.

In 1946, Los Angeles International Airport began operations with five commercial carriers offering regularly scheduled domestic and international service. There were by that time five incorporated areas around the airport: Westchester to the north, Inglewood to the northeast, Lennox to the east, Hawthorne to the southeast, and El Segundo to the south. Each of these communities was prospering and, with the end of the war and subsequent re-laxation of controls placed on building materials, each was enjoying an un-precedented building boom. With each new housing development, the dis-tance between the end of the airport runways and the residential areas was decreasing. As that distance decreased, complaints increased. However, the complaints lacked the clout of consensus and the number of them was not sufficient to generate any strong public reaction. Los Angeles and the rest of America were enjoying the relative calm and prosperity of the postwar era.

At the national level, however, airports had become the subject of several congressional discussions. At the end of World War II, the federal government declared some 500 airports surplus. These had been constructed for the military by the Civil Aeronautics Authority. As the CAA in its wartime con-struction programs had attempted to consider the requirements of postwar civil aviation, the majority of the fields were suitable for transfer to local authorities which could operate them as municipal airports. Congress, recognizing the importance of aviation to national defense, passed a bill which allowed the federal government, in conjunction with the state or local municipalities, to continue an airport construction program. The bill gave the federal government a larger role in airport regulation. At the same time, some of the more alert members of the administration recognized that the untrammeled growth of the civil aivation industry must now be brought under control. Commercial passen-ger traffic had reached an unforeseen level, and several aircraft accidents had left the public clamoring for increased safety measures at airports.

Several committees were set up to study the airport problem, but the one which received the greatest attention was the Doolittle Committee of 1952. Its report contained several items that should have been heeded by all com-munities where major airports were being developed. The report stated prophet-ically that community encroachment on the airports would prove to be a major problem for future airport improvement efforts. The abnormal wartime growth of populations in communities contingent to airports and the unabated increase in airport noise would elicit public pressure, which in turn could jeopardize the airports and the large investments of public and private funds they represented.

It is difficult to tell whether Los Angeles city administrators read the Doolittle report and grasped the potential problems it identified. With the rapid growth of Los Angeles International Airport traffic, Los Angeles needed to expand the airport's facilities. At the same time, the number of complaints was increasing. By 1954, residential areas had sprung up on the northern perimeter of the airport. The houses in this subdivision were built within reading distance of signs warning that future construction plans for the airport called for a runway to be built along the northern perimeter.

On December 8, 1957, the city held a ground-breaking ceremony for an expansion program to prepare Los Angeles International Airport for the jet age. No public demonstration protested the expansion. In fact, the mayor of Los Angeles, civic leaders, and more than 200 students from various schools and organizations took part in the ceremony. Sand from Kitty Hawk, North Carolina, was brought in and mixed with the airport soil in symbolic recognition of the historical significance of the day: the ceremony implied that the advent of the jet age to Los Angeles was an event as commemorable as the Wright brothers' first powered flight.

In retrospect, it is easy to understand what was happening. The aerospace industry in the Los Angeles area was still expanding. Only two days earlier, the first American-built, commercial turboprop, the Lockheed Electra, had been test flown in the Los Angeles area. In addition, estimates had just been released that more than 50 percent of the employed population of Los Angeles was directly or indirectly associated with the aerospace industry. Aviation was sovereign!

The jet age at Los Angeles International Airport became a reality in January 1959, when the first commercial jet began one regularly scheduled round-trip per day. Within six months, there were twelve regularly scheduled round-trips a day in and out of Los Angeles. And as rapidly as the jet traffic grew, so did complaints from the residential area. Still, no legal actions were taken. By 1963, the traffic at LAX had increased so quickly that airport authorities began planning further expansion. The work for it began in 1967; and, at the same time, the northern runway was opened to jet traffic, on a limited basis. The action brought a fury of complaints. Although airport authorities attempted to appease their neighbors, they were not successful. In August 1968, a citizen group from Inglewood filed a $1.4 billion suit against the Los Angeles International Airport for damage to property values, health, safety, and the welfare of the community. That action opened a new phase for the airport. Within three years' time, more than forty suits asking for about $3 billion from the airport were filed. In 1971, a California superior court awarded damages in the amount of $659,440 to 520 local landowners. The amount was upheld by the U.S. Supreme Court in January 1975.

In the decade since Los Angeles began its preparation for the jet age, much had happened. First of all, the communities of Los Angeles had achieved a level of prosperity high enough to allow time for leisure and reflection; economic considerations were no longer the primary motivating factors of citizen behavior. Irritants which had previously been accepted because they were by-products of welcomed industrial operations were now being rejected. The aerospace industry in the Los Angeles area was proportionally declining and its share of the employed population was decreasing. City and county administrations had accommodated engineering changes to facilitate the new technology, but they had failed to make adjustments to lessen the environmental impact of those changes. Regulation of the carriers had been left to the federal government, which was still moving slowly in the environmental area. The louder noise from larger jets increased the radius of the residential areas affected, giving the opposition a greater power base. And, of course, the civil air industry had not regulated itself enough to fulfill its social as well as its economic obligations.

After the fact, both the Los Angeles administration and the state legislature tried to institute measures to correct the problems. The earliest gesture made was to establish a noise abatement program. The new Airport Sound Abatement Coordinating Committee, funded jointly by the airport and the airlines, set up requirements which included flying slightly above the prescribed altitude of the glide slope when approaching those runways equipped with instrument landing systems, staying above 2,000 feet in the visual flight rules traffic pattern until turning into the final approach, using a westerly flow of traffic for takeoffs and landings so that operations would be mostly over the Pacific, and restricting jet aircraft use of the north runways between 10 P.M. and 6 A.M. These requirements were not popular with the carriers inasmuch as they reduced operational efficiency and safety. When even this program failed to satisfy the public, the airport authorities began buying land around the airport to increase the distance between runways and residential areas. Approximately $70 million was spent to acquire 2,500 homes, some of which were razed while others were left standing. The measure was not really successful. Not only had it been expensive, but in those areas where the houses had been torn down, neighbors outside the "buy zone" complained that their level of noise had increased as a direct consequence. The houses still standing became a haven for vandals and rats. In those areas where homeowners were not bought out, attempts were made to soundproof the houses. The cost of modifying a house ranged between $3,000 and $12,000. In short, the program has had little success.

Because the noise abatement programs tried so far were failures, Los Angeles city officials decided to purchase 17,000 acres of desert land at Palmdale to provide the city with another airport. The purchase of the land was promptly challenged by the Sierra Club in the courts. It appears that the suit will delay construction and increase costs by as much as a billion dollars. Here again there is to be no happy solution in the immediate future.

Bibliography

Horonjeff, Robert. *Planning and Design of Airports*, New York: McGraw-Hill, 1969.

Hunter, F.S. "LAX Studies Housing Insulation as Way to Decrease Jet Noise."
    American Aviation, 16 September 1968, p. 66.
Hunter, G.S. "Los Angeles Moves to Meet Traffic Gains." *Aviation Weekly*,
    17 July 1967, p. 55.
Los Angeles Times, 1929 to 1975.
New York Times, January 1930 through September 1975.
Parris, R.L. "LA Girds for Jet-Noise Showdown." *American Aviation*,
    6 January 1969, p. 23.
Ropelewski, R.R. "Traffic Growth, Noise Wrack LA Airport Planning."
    Aviation Weekly, 15 November 1971, p. 74.

4

San Francisco's Transportation Problems: The Freeway Revolt and the BART Controversy

San Francisco is considered one of America's finest cities—the center of a region of highly desirable real estate. The city's geographic location provides much of its inherent appeal. Located at the tip of a peninsula, San Francisco wraps around three steep hills—Nob, Telegraph, and Russian. The hills provide strikingly beautiful vistas for virtually all of the central city. The moderate Pacific breezes give the entire San Francisco Bay area a pleasant, even climate throughout the year. Temperatures in the sixties, summer and winter, allow San Franciscans to dress for style rather than the climate.

San Francisco Bay, with its spectacular Golden Gate and San Francisco–Oakland Bay bridges, adds to the area's aesthetic qualities. The city's fine harbor is a center for trade between the United States and lands throughout the Pacific basin from Alaska to New Zealand.

San Francisco's location has helped it become a major financial, business, and governmental center on the West Coast. With its regional stock exchange, Montgomery Street is known as the Wall Street of the West. Major firms—such as Bank of America, the Transamerica Corporation, and the Southern Pacific Transportation Company—are headquartered in its densely developed central business district.

San Francisco's location and topography make it unique. At the same time, the city's transportation problems are severe because of its unique situation. The famous hills and narrow peninsula have fostered intensive development, leaving no easy routes for transportation arteries. To sustain the dense urban environment, a full and efficient transportation service must be provided for large numbers of people. The fact that the center city is encircled on three sides by transportation barriers, the ocean and the bay, compounds the problem. Philadelphia and New York are the only other major American cities with as many natural barriers.

From its famous cable-car lines to its present heavy rail rapid transit system, San Francisco has faced some unusually difficult urban transportation problems and has addressed them with admirable ingenuity. Because it was the first of the heavy rail rapid transit systems developed in the United States in the past fifty years, and because complete data collection is made relatively easy by the wide publicity the Bay Area Rapid Transit (BART) has received, the BART system makes an attractive case study. The Washington, D.C., and Atlanta systems are modeled on San Francisco's BART.

The San Francisco Freeway Revolt

Transportation decisions, like other decision-making processes, require the formulation of goals and of long-range plans to implement those goals. On December 20, 1945, the San Francisco City Planning Commission adopted plans for freeways, parkways, rapid transit, and off-street parking in the Transportation and Utilities Section of a City Master Plan. That plan has been cited as the first long-range, comprehensive transportation plan for the area. In reality, it was more an interim than a comprehensive plan because it recommended another, more complete study of the city's transportation system. Based on the master plan's recommendations the city planning commission appropriated $200,000 for a transportation survey to be conducted by the Transportation Technical Committee, appointed by the mayor of San Francisco to represent the Department of City Planning, the Department of Public Works, the Public Utilities Commission, and the Police Department. Perhaps because these agencies are supposed to operate for the benefit of the citizens, the mayor neglected to provide for any direct citizen participation in the committee. In November 1948, the Transportation Technical Committee published the *Report to the City Planning Commission on a Transportation Plan for San Francisco.*

The report recommended a coordinated system of freeways, expressways, parkways, major and secondary thoroughfares, rail line subways, bus subways, a completely modernized program of traffic control, a large-scale program of downtown off-street parking facilities, and a revised citywide land-use plan. Public hearings were held and completed, and the commission's plan (known as the Traffic-Ways Plan) was formally adopted in July 1951. Because of its general nature and distant eventuality, not much controversy arose at the time.

But community reaction was not far in the future. After California's Collier-Burns Act was passed in 1948, increasing the state gasoline tax to provide additional funds for improving the state's highway system, proposed freeways began to be built and the "freeway revolt" began. As funds became available between the years 1949 to 1955, studies and surveys were made of the Western, Junipero-Serra, and Park-Presidio freeways in San Francisco. When it became apparent that the proposed freeways would cross the Golden Gate Park panhandle, nearby residents and the Parks and Recreation Commission feared the Golden Gate Park would be irreparably damaged. Responding to community reaction, the Parks and Recreation Commission passed a resolution on January 21, 1955, opposing a freeway through the panhandle, any aboveground crossing over the park, and the use of park property for any use other than park purposes. The City Planning Commission then deleted, pending further study, those parts of the Traffic-Ways Plan which involved the use of park property, while state engineers proposed alternative routes crossing the residential area just south of the park panhandle.

The Western Freeway continued to attract attention as property owners in the area and park officials became involved. A group of neighborhood clubs invited the Division of Highways to explain its plans at a public meeting on December 2, 1955, at Lincoln High School. Over 2,000 property owners and interested citizens attended the meeting. The Division of Highways, as it happened, was ill-prepared to answer all the questions about the various routes under consideration. This led to accusations of official secrecy. Many citizens felt that they were deliberately being kept in the dark and that their property values might be endangered.

Other neighborhood groups, such as the Haight-Asbury district's United Neighborhood Alliance and the Glen Park Residents, banded together to fight the proposed freeways on the grounds that freeways required too much property, degraded the neighborhoods, required unattractive structures, and destroyed neighborhood business centers.

On April 27, 1956, over 1,600 people opposed to the Western Freeway gathered at Lincoln High School, and six weeks later, on June 11, 1956, the San Francisco Board of Supervisors echoed the citizens' sentiments by passing a resolution opposing the construction of the Western Freeway. In 1957, however, state highway officials insisted that the Western Freeway was a link essential to the state and national highway systems, that it would provide a vital connection between the Golden Gate Bridge and the rapidly developing towns to the south, and that it would service commuters in the suburbs to the south and west of San Francisco. The Board of Supervisors then reversed its previous stand on the Western Freeway and authorized a $45,000 survey to determine whether the Western Freeway was really necessary and, if so, to recommend the route it should take. On December 17, 1957, after $45,000 and one year's time had been spent taking traffic counts, making origin-designation surveys, conducting personal interviews, and performing sophisticated analyses, the consultants submitted their report, which stated that the Western Freeway would be a necessity within ten years. The report recommended a route essentially the same as the 1951 Traffic-Ways Plan had projected. Essentially, the status of the Western Freeway, to the chagrin of many, remained unchanged.

The Embarcadero Freeway, included in the 1948 and 1951 plans, was probably the most controversial freeway—especially after five new developments changed the original plans for it. First, traffic estimates taken by the Division of Highways indicated that an eight-lane double-deck structure would be necessary. Second, the proposed underpass at the Ferry Building, designed to preserve the beauty of that landmark and its surrounding area, was determined to be $15 million more expensive than the $9 million elevated structure. The exorbitant cost ruled out the underpass scheme. Third, the eighteen-block area lying north of Market Street and west of the Embarcadero was selected for redevelopment as an apartment and office-tower complex to be named the Golden Gateway, and the proposed elevated freeway was unwelcome along the eastern boundary of the redevelopment area. Fourth, part of the projected

redevelopment efforts was to create a state park near the Ferry Building, but the
State Park Commission would not accept these plans because of the proximity of
a double-deck freeway. Finally, despite all objections, the Division of Highways
designed and built a structure so unnecessarily ugly that its appearance was almost universally condemned.

Fearing they had not seen the worst, citizen opposition grew more vocifer-
ous, until on January 23, 1959, the San Francisco Board of Supervisors registered
the public sentiment in Resolution Number 45-59. The resolution voiced the
board's opposition to the construction of all the freeways proposed in the San
Francisco Master Plan, including the Western, Junipero-Serra, and Park-Presidio
freeways, the Central Freeway from Turk Street to its connection with the
Golden Gate Freeway, the entire Golden Gate Freeway from Embarcadero and
Bay Street to the Golden Gate Bridge, the Mission Freeway from Thirteenth
Street to its connection with the Southern Freeway, and the Embarcadero
Freeway.

Given the elimination of all future freeway construction while freeway congestion was continuing to grow, San Francisco's transportation hopes lay in the
development of a high-speed, high-capacity heavy rail rapid transit system. Most
of the rapid transit planning in the bay area prior to the Second World War had
focused primarily on limited subway systems for the San Francisco central
business district. Before the war, San Francisco's voters evidently did not share
the enthusiasm of the city's commercial leaders. They rejected a subway proposal in the November 1937 election. During World War II, however, the
strategic importance of traffic movement to national security prompted the
federal government to create an Army-Navy Board to study the need for additional Bay crossings. The joint board recommended a completely integrated
rapid transit system with a subaqueous tube between San Francisco and Oakland. The idea of rapid transit for San Francisco thus underwent a radical shift.
No longer a local concern articulated by local elites and downtown businessmen,
it was now a regional wartime issue in which federal authorities were interested.

Civic leaders were alarmed because consumer buying patterns were shifting
outward, from the central city to the new, lower-cost suburbs. Moreover, during peak commuting hours, traffic congestion at the six principal gateways to
San Francisco was growing, discouraging many consumers from making their
way into the inner city. The solution to the problems of traffic congestion and
business area rejuvenation seemed to be a high-speed, high-capacity heavy rail
system operating on its own right-of-way.

In 1949, the California State Legislature approved the formation of a rapid
transit district encompassing various local governments in the San Francisco
metropolitan area. The purpose of the legislation was to promote domestic
and international trade which would benefit the state by allowing maximum use
of the San Francisco Harbor. Since rapid transit would provide access to the
harbor, state funds spent on this particular local project would naturally benefit
the state as well

In 1951, Governor Earl Warren signed a bill setting up the San Francisco Bay Area Rapid Transit Commission to examine the city's transportation problem. The commission's report to the legislature, made in 1953, suggested (1) that a satisfactory solution to the transit problem required more than automobile facilities alone; (2) that the Bay Area needed a coordinated system of mass rapid transit operating on its own rights-of-way; and (3) that a master, coordinated rapid transit plan should be developed by one central agency because individual communities were not equipped to do the job well themselves.

The BART Controversy

In early 1957, Senator John F. McCarthy of Marin County sponsored a commission-drafted version of a bill to create a rapid transit district, and in June 1957, the legislature constituted the Bay Area Rapid Transit District. It was hoped BART would (1) preserve and enhance urban centers and subcenters; (2) increase property values; (3) help prevent disorganized urban sprawl; (4) improve employment conditions, because mass transit facilities would attract industry; (5) improve access to social, cultural, and recreational opportunities; and (6) generally provide low-cost transportation.

Good as this might seem, there was immediate speculation that the interest of public planners in fixed rail systems was traceable to a preference for systems entirely within their control, so that they could sidestep any need to deal with or rely on highway builders and managers.

The transit district was composed initially of five of the nine Bay area counties: Alameda and Contra Costa in the East Bay; Marin, which is west and north of the bay; and San Francisco and San Mateo, west of the Bay. The legislation made provisions for other counties to annex to the district, but, more importantly, any of the original counties could withdraw from BART by a vote of the county supervisors to do so.

The original plans for BART comprehended a 120-mile system at a cost of $792 million. The completed system was to be much shorter and much more expensive. BART was to be the nation's first modern regional rapid transit system unique in its ability to operate without a deficit by using laborsaving automation.

The trains, manufactured by Rohr Industries, were to run over a total of seventy-five miles of track: twenty-seven miles of surface track, twenty-five miles of elevated lines, nineteen miles of subways, and four miles of earthquake-proof tunnel under the Bay. The trains were to be completely automated and run by a computer. Each train was to have one attendant present for emergency situations. The trains would achieve speeds of up to 80 mph and passengers would be issued magnetically coded tickets instead of coins or tokens. The first trains were planned to run in 1967, with the completed system ready by 1971. Plagued by many problems and controversies, BART officially opened on November 3,

1973, after fifteen years of planning and eight years of construction. The trans-Bay tube did not open until September 16, 1974.

Once it was operative, purely mechanical problems caused about 30 percent of the cars to be removed from service and repaired each day. Five persons were injured only one month after operations began, when the computerized braking system failed and one of the cars went off the end of the track in Fremont, California. BART was stalled for twenty-seven days in 1973, when 1,100 of BART's 1,375 employees went on strike for fair wages.

But BART's delay in opening and its costliness were results not of mechanical and organizational problems alone, but of community-provoked controversy.

The controversy stirred up by BART and subsequent community actions proved more costly, in terms of both time and money, than the construction-related problems. Four types of community-generated controversy can be isolated for analysis—objections can be principally political, economic, legal, or aesthetic.

Political Controversy

Political controversy arose as early as 1959 when BART's financial consultants, Smith, Barney & Company of New York, recommended to the state legislature that the construction of the subaqueous trans-Bay tube be financed from Bay Bridge toll revenues. Legislative approval was apparently given for two reasons. First, the State Division of Highways wanted to remove the Key System train tracks from the Bay Bridge and convert the space to thoroughfares for vehicular traffic only. This plan was presumably supported by entities behind the highway lobby. Second, if the train tracks were removed and BART bond election failed, the prospects for a southern bridge across the Bay, which the Highway Department wanted badly, would be greatly enhanced. The BART bond election was to be in excess of $500 million, and most politicians thought the electorate would not approve a measure of that magnitude.

Later, the state legislature became involved again—this time to determine whether those appointed to the BART board of directors could concurrently hold elected political offices. By law, members of the BART board are appointed by conferences of city mayors and county supervisors. The state's attorney general held that no one holding an elected public office could serve concurrently as a director of BART. The League of California Cities and the California Supervisors Association disagreed with the attorney general's finding and actively sought to change it. In January 1961, assemblyman Jerome Waldie of Contra Costa County introduced a bill that, if passed, would give local political officials more control over the affairs of the transit district. The bill would also remove the eastern portion of Contra Costa County from the transit district which vowed to support the system with tax monies. BART officials, opposed to the

Waldie bill but aware of the support it had for passage, attempted to kill it with
Senate Bill 639, introduced by Senator John McCarthy of Marin County. In
essence, McCarthy's bill reduced the affirmative votes necessary to approve the
forthcoming BART bond issue from 66 2/3 percent to just 60 percent. Despite
the efforts of BART officials, the Waldie bill passed—but McCarthy's amend-
ment also passed. Had the McCarthy bill not passed, the 1962 bond election
would have been defeated since the bond issue scraped by with a 61.215 percent majority.

As mentioned earlier, the counties belonging to the transit district could
withdraw if the county supervisors elected to do so or if the voters decided in a
general election to withdraw. The plan for BART was formally submitted to
each of the five boards of supervisors in October 1961. San Mateo County's
board of supervisors not only rejected the BART plan but made it clear that
no rapid transit plan would be satisfactory. The reasons for San Mateo's withdrawal are unclear, but newspaper accounts give four apparent reasons. First,
the costs to county taxpayers for the system were thought to exceed the benefits,
seen in terms of facilities located within the county. Second, the Southern
Pacific was already operating an effective rail-commuter service from the peninsula to San Francisco, and BART would only duplicate the existing service.
Third, in order to pay for the system, property taxes would have to increase
substantially. Fourth, most people using the rapid transit system would still
need to drive to and from the sparsely located BART stations.

The withdrawal of San Mateo County had serious implications for the
remaining counties, most particularly for Marin County. Because of its low
population density and rough terrain, the cost of providing rapid transit to
Marin County would exceed the county's bonding capacity. San Mateo County
had excess bonding capacity, but when it withdrew, BART lost the cushion
of resources that was to be used to construct the Marin County segment of the
system. BART officials therefore requested that Marin County also withdraw
from the system. The request was refused by the Marin County board of
supervisors. In 1961, BART eventually got its way when the Golden Gate
Bridge supervisors rejected a proposal for the operation of rapid transit trains
on a lower deck to be added to the Golden Gate Bridge. There was no other
easy way for rapid transit trains to cross the mouth of the Bay and serve
Marin County. Isolated from the system by the decision, Marin County reluctantly withdrew from the transit district. The exit of both San Mateo and Marin
counties dealt a serious blow since it removed the highly populated peninsula,
San Francisco International Airport, and a major county from the system.

Next, when the Contra Costa County supervisors voted, two were for the
system and two were against it, with one undecided. Objections stemmed
from the fact that BART would not serve most of the country, while all the
taxpayers would have to be taxed to pay for the system. The political process
then began to steamroll. The undecided supervisor was pressured by the

governor, the mayor of San Francisco, and the BART board members. Yielding to the pressure tactics of government, he decided to allow the electorate to vote on whether they wanted the systems or not. Later, he was elected to BART's board of directors.

Economic Controversy

The conflict over the bond election was basically a financial one. The primary support for BART came from the business community, particularly from the larger chambers of commerce and the Bay Area Council. An effective areawide advertising and fund-raising campaign was launched, and the four largest newspapers in the region advocated an affirmative vote on the BART bonds. Nonetheless, the BART bond issue still generated considerable opposition. At $792 million, the BART bond issue was the largest ever submitted to voters at the local level. The general-obligation bonds proposed amounted to thirteen times the total transit indebtedness in the state at that time. Furthermore the bond issue election was being held in California, 2,000 miles from nearest existing rapid transit system, where partisans of the private automobile and the expanding network of freeways in combination with the highway lobby were considered almost unbeatable enemies. Surprisingly, no organized opposition developed, although the city councils of Albany and Antioch, the Alameda County Taxpayers' Association, and the Contra Costa Farm Bureau went on record against approving the BART bonds.

Proposition A called for the issuance of $792 million worth of general-obligation bonds for construction of the basic system. The $121 million needed for the trans-Bay tube would be acquired from tolls on traffic from three auto bridges in the area, and the $149 million needed to build the cars would be paid from revenues from operations. In order to get approval on the first vote, the BART board promised the cities that certain changes could be made after the election, a statement that would later come to haunt them. As previously stated, the bond issue, which had to obtain at least a 60 percent majority of affirmative votes, was passed by a mere 61.215 percent.

Legal Controversy

Only one week after the bond election had taken place a third source of controversy arose. The legality of the transit district was challenged in a taxpayers' suit instituted in a state superior court against BART and the joint-venture engineers Parsons, Brinckerhoff, Tudor, and Bechtel (PBTB). This taxpayers' suit was brought against BART by four citizens: Messrs. Nunn, Gertsch, Osborne, an Oakland City councilman, and Boblitt, the mayor of El Cerrito. The plaintiffs challenged the legality of the transit district, of the 60 percent special bond issue provision, of the election, and of the engineering agreement with PBTB.

Friendly suits are often initiated against public works projects as a means of guaranteeing legitimacy and legality. But in this instance it was clear that the suit was not friendly. The specific allegations of the case were that the bond election should be invalidated on the grounds that transit district funds were being used to finance a campaign supporting it and that the public was being misled by that campaign. The suit challenged the engineering contract for $47,250,000 with PBTB, alleging that it was entered into improperly and that some of the transit district's personnel were hired improperly. The suit lasted eight months. The transit district had been enjoined from issuing the bonds authorized in November and therefore had to stop preliminary engineering work on the trans-Bay tube and other surface planning until the trial was completed. There were those who contended that the taxpayers' suit was a tactic to destroy the project by costly delays. But the court acquitted both BART and PBTB of having engaged in any illegalities, and the case was closed on June 10, 1963, when construction began.

Aesthetics

A high standard of quality in construction and design of the BART system was considered a basic condition from the start. BART was not to be like the earlier, more conventional systems of heavy rail found in northeastern cities. Indeed, PBTB stated in their *Transit Vehicle System Evaluation and Recommendation*, issued in 1963, that the major drawback to a bottom-supported, flanged-wheel, duo-rail system was its association in the mind of the general public with the crowded rapid transit and subway lines of eastern cities. The design chosen for the BART system was to reflect modern, state-of-the-art concepts as much as possible. It was believed that one line of controversy—the criticism that the system was not advanced enough to justify its huge expense—might thus be avoided. The designers' emphasis on technological attainment led to their adoption of an automatic control system and of a nonstandard track gauge of five feet six inches. It was hoped that these design elements would given voters a better image of BART, thereby gaining support for BART bonds.

The high standards for design were not limited to matters of technology, but extended to the environmental and aesthetic aspects of the system as well. Air and water pollution are rarely generated in great quantities by an electric-powered rail system; it is the power generation facility, generally not associated directly with the system, which may or may not create these problems. Noise and ugliness are, of course, products of a heavy rail system. The PBTB design group pointed out the relative benignity of its modern system, and this reduced controversy over pollution and increased the acceptability of the system to its future users.

The noise a heavy rail system generates is less than and different from freeway noise. Unlike the steady sounds of tires on concrete pavement, of the various sorts of engines, and of whooshing wind stirred up by big trucks, rail noise is intermittent, limited to the small percentage of time trains take to pass over a given stretch of track. Electric propulsion eliminates engine noises, leaving only wheel-track contact noises and the squeal of the braking systems. While the traditional clickety-clack of the steel wheel passing over rail joints is not usually objectionable, the noise created when trains run over an elevated structure, as they do in New York, Chicago, and a number of other cities, is clearly a problem. Elevated structures, usually giant steel trestles erected over a city street, act as sounding boards for the noises of wheel-track interaction and do nothing to dampen the loud squeals created by metal brake shoes against steel wheels during braking.

In order to give a high level of service, noise levels inside the rail cars had to be reduced to a level which would draw commuters from their automobiles onto the trains. External noise levels, in the case of BART, were of somewhat secondary importance, due to the nature of most of the rights-of-way. The lower the external sound levels, of course, the less insulation was required to keep those noises out of the car interiors.

BART was designed to incorporate numerous noise abatement features, beginning with the use of a continuous welded rail to eliminate the clickety-clack. The roadbed between the rails was acoustically designed to absorb noises made by the running gear and brakes. These noises were further reduced by using a low-noise brake system and an acoustically designed wheel. A good part of the remaining noise was confined beneath the cars by deep side-skirts along the bottom of each car side. To reduce vibration, resilient mountings were used between the rails and their base, between the equipment and the trucks, and between the chassis and the trucks. To further reduce exterior noise, trackside sound barriers—trees and shrubs, fences and walls, and earthwork berms—were devised. What little noise remained was further reduced in the interior by an insulated body shell and permanently closed windows, made possible by air conditioning.

Since the actual roadbed of BART could be as narrow as twenty-six feet, the visual-aesthetic problems of the trackage were clearly less than they might have been for a multilaned freeway or even for a major arterial street, which typically varies from forty-four to ninety-six feet in total width. When located at grade, the low height and intensity of construction permitted the trackwork to be easily overlooked. Modern structural technology allows elevated structures to be long-span concrete beams supported by single pillar abutments, a great improvement over traditional elevated rapid transit design. The light-colored concrete trestlework, as narrow as possible, with an opening between the tracks to admit sunlight into the center of the structure, reflected underneath it, eliminating much of the dark, dreary shadows created by a normal elevated construction.

The rolling stock was designed to look modern as well as to incorporate the newest rail transit technology. The cars were made a pleasing blend of stainless steel and glass, trimmed in blue. They were to be equally attractive to riders encountering them in the stations and to spectators viewing them at speed from a distance.

BART's various right-of-way locations provided different visual situations. Where BART ran at grade level, it was often located in the median of a freeway, and visual separation was provided by the road. If it was located elsewhere, walls, fences, berms, or landscaping were used to help conceal the train route. Elevated structures cannot be as easily hidden, and therefore in several cases the land beneath the structure and the adjacent right of way were turned into a linear park to mitigate the adverse impact of the structure on surrounding neighborhoods.

In keeping with the overall philosophy of the project, the BART designers assumed that the Bay Area population would desire station structures which were not merely attractive but distinctive, reflecting the character of the town or neighborhood they served. The designs for each station were individually drawn up, with systemwide standardization of functional elements only, like platform height and length, track separation, and platform width.

Despite the excellent design work, a central issue arose regarding the type of construction chosen for San Francisco's new heavy rail system. Subways are thought clearly superior to surface construction of either the at-grade or elevated variety. The choice between the latter two types largely involves a trade-off between the higher cost of elevated construction versus the reduced accessibility across the rail line inherent in at-grade construction. While below-grade construction is mandated by certain types of right-of-way restrictions (primarily the difficulty of acquiring sufficient space for elevated station structures), in many cases it is simply a higher-quality, higher-cost substitute for elevated construction. Even with the extensive planning and first-class design which were features of the Bay area system, the BART district authorities encountered serious controversy over the choice between subway and elevated construction in the East Bay city of Berkeley.

In the initial feasibility study, *Regional Rapid Transit: A Report to the San Francisco Bay Area Rapid Transit Commission, 1953-55*, done by Parsons, Brinckerhoff, Hall and MacDonald, the system was roughed out with respect to basic route location and type of construction. Their plan called for a route through the center of Berkeley, passing on a north-south alignment, taking a route through the heart of the central business district. The plan called for three stations: one in the north, one in the south, and one in the central business district. Due to the desire to keep construction costs at a minimum, the structure in Berkeley was to be elevated all the way.

Despite the modern design of the aerial structure, the prevailing sentiment in Berkeley was that the elevated trackway running through the center of the city would be unattractive. Berkeleyans also believed that the elevated structure would create a barrier, not physical but sociological, between the east and west parts of the town. In response to local sentiment, the Berkeley City Council passed a resolution in 1960 requesting that all BART facilities within the city limits be underground. The transit district administrators rejected the resolution, holding that the cost differential was too great to substitute below-grade for elevated construction. If BART had yielded to Berkeley's request, not only would the city have received a disproportionally large share of the funds available for rapid transit construction in the East Bay area, but the action might have set a precedent for every city along the line to request below-grade construction, escalating costs to the point where the system would have had to be greatly reduced in length.

The Parsons, Brinckerhoff, Tudor, Bechtel document *The Composite Report: Bay Area Rapid Transit*, released in 1962, did finally concede a short stretch of subway in the downtown area and an underground station in the central business district. Despite continuing plans for the remaining trackage to be elevated, in November 1962 Berkeley voters supported the BART bond issue.

Three members of the Berkeley City Council constituted the transit committee. They were Mayor Wallace Johnson, Councilman Wilmont Sweeney, and Joseph Bort. In order to continue to push for complete underground facilities, they requested estimates from BART district officials in July 1963 as to the comparative costs of aerial and subway construction. In March 1964, the transit district administrators released figures of approximately $2.5 million per mile for elevated trackage and $10 million per mile for subway. When Berkeley's transit committee asked for some justifications to back up these figures, the BART district engineers refused to give cost breakdowns. Berkeley's transit committee next took steps to secure an independent estimate of the costs and to get the BART district board to hear its case.

The cost estimates were derived from the experiences of two Canadian cities, Toronto and Montreal, where the most recent comparable subway construction projects had been located. The hearings before the BART district board were made possible by a provision in the act creating the transit district. It stated that any county or city having territory located within the transit district may file a request for a hearing before the transit district board to contest the location of facilities by transit engineers.

In a hearing held in the spring of 1964, the board backed its own engineers and their cost estimate of $22 million per mile, against the $11 million per mile the Berkeley Transit Committee presented as a reasonable cost.

The discrepancy between the BART district and Berkeley estimates received wide local publicity. The public pressure and uncertainty forced the two parties to reach a compromise.

The city of Berkeley and the BART district agreed in the fall of 1964 to solicit bids on the two alternative plans, a part below-grade, part elevated construction and an all below-grade facility, with the city of Berkeley allowed to execute as much of the additional below-grade construction (beyond the amount allowed in the 1962 *Composite Report*) as it was willing to pay for. While this was, in principle, the final agreement, the BART district staff continued to harass the Berkeley group with inflated cost estimates throughout the following two years. The situation nearly caused the failure of the entire agreement when in 1966, immediately prior to a bond election in Berkeley which was to finance the subway construction, the two sides could not agree on a figure for the bond issue. The BART district officials wanted to post a figure in excess of $25 million, while the Berkeley groups believed that the additional cost of construction should only run about $16.5 million. Berkeley chose to yield to the district, and the election was set for October 4, 1964.

The campaign to pass the bond issue was intense. The major point in conflict was whether the elevated structure would create a significant division of the city of Berkeley. The major fear was that a division would split Berkeley along racial lines, a polarization the city as a whole rejected. The persistence of city officials finally paid off. More than 80 percent of the voters voted in favor of the proposal, despite the additional taxes the city would be required to levy in order to pay for the improvement.

Currently, BART trains run underground throughout Berkeley, serving the growing central business district through an underground station which is surrounded by new office buildings and shops, whose development was encouraged by their access to BART service.

While the Berkeley example does show how controversy can arise about the location of heavy rail transit lines, the physical problem was easily solved. The real controversy stemmed from the kinds of relationships that sprang up between the local group, the citizens of Berkeley, the regional bureaucracy, and the Bay Area Transit District. Wallace Johnson, former Berkeley mayor and member of its transit committee, summarizes the controversy in his book *Responsible Individualism: Perspectives on a Political Philosophy for Our Time*. He observed that public opinion coalesced into the view that Berkeley should settle for a short subway line and not obstruct the regional staff's plans unnecessarily.

Conclusion

As can be seen in this case, San Francisco is a significant example of urban transportation problems encountered in both the highway and rail modes. The community has been in the forefront of the recent developments and, as a consequence, has endured the problems associated with innovation. As San Francisco has seen controversy over both freeways and rail systems, it provides an especially interesting case, showing the contrasts between the kinds of controversies each mode stirs.

Relatively early, San Francisco generated opposition to freeway construction. The physical effects on the aesthetic and social environments were the central issues. Plans for the Embarcadero Freeway showed San Franciscans how environmentally disruptive a poorly designed expressway could be. Sufficient citizen opposition was easily aroused for the other proposed major freeway segments, as they tried to cut through parkland or invade neighborhoods. On the other hand, the heavy rail BART system avoided this controversy because seventy miles of its eighty-five-mile length were located either underground, requiring no surface right-of-way, or along existing transportation corridors, such as in freeway medians or along railroad lines.

The BART system did not have a preexisting, statewide agency for its construction, maintenance, and operation, as the state freeway system had the California Department of Highways. In the Bay area, much of the controversy surrounding BART was associated with the creation of the special taxation and operating agency, the Bay Area Rapid Transit District. As an intermediate-level entity—smaller than the state yet larger than the cities and counties—the BART district faced a number of problems in dealing with the various local governments.

Funding for the rail system was controversial because the entire construction cost burden was placed on the three counties comprising the district. The state's freeway system, which was constructed using only 10 percent state funds, placed a much smaller burden per capita on local taxpayers. Ninety percent of the funds for freeway construction were provided by the federal government.

Even though marked differences exist, some parallels can be drawn among the controversial aspects of both modes. One of the most unfortunate and costly of the problems involved the resistance of governmental agencies to objections voiced by the general public. Only after persistent efforts to make themselves heard were local sentiments considered by bureaucratic organizations charged with construction, whether of rail rapid transit systems or highways. When public opinion was finally heeded, freeway-building was stopped in San Francisco and BART was built underground in Berkeley. But these developments came only after the controversy was pursued for long periods by concerned neighborhood citizens and diligent local officials. It should not require such great efforts to initiate changes on public works which impact upon so many people.

Finally, it can be seen that aesthetic and social considerations can be of major importance. The most heated controversies arising in relation to this case history centered about these intangible factors. The moral is that the best systems blend in with their environment; those which do not cause the most uproar.

Bibliography

"BART Remolds Cities." *Christian Science Monitor*, Eastern Edition, 16 May 1968, p. 3.

"Bring Back Ferries Talk." *Chirstian Science Monitor*, Eastern Edition, 8 July 1966, p. 1.

EBASCO Service Incorporated. *Rapid Transit System Economic Review.* San Francisco, 1961.

Roberson, Charles E. *San Francisco Bay Area Rapid Transit District: A Description and an Analysis of its Benefits and Costs.* Unpublished professional report, University of Texas at Austin, 1969.

Shepard, Lyn. "Revolt Leaps Forward." Part 3 of 10-part series on urban freeways, *Christian Science Monitor,* 11 June 1968, p. 3.

Simpson and Curtin Consulting Engineers. *Coordinated Transit for the San Francisco Bay Area, Now to 1975.* Philadelphia, 1967.

Stokes, B.R. "What Can Others Learn From BART." *Railway Age*, April 1968, p. 26-27.

"Taxpayers Suit Seen Stalling BART." *New York Times*, 6 March 1963, p. 11.

"Three S.F. Bay Area Counties to Hold Bond Election." *New York Times,* 29 July 1962, p. 50.

"Transit Hits Snag in California." *Railway Age*, September 1967, pp. 22-23.

Weiss, Wayne. "BART–Its Political Problems." Student paper done for Dr. Henry M. Steiner, 5 January 1969.

Zettel, Richard M. *Urban Transportation in the San Francisco Bay Area.* Berkeley: Institute of Governmental Studies, University of California, 1974.

Zwerling, Stephen. *Mass Transit and the Politics of Technology: A Study of BART and the San Francisco Bay Area.* New York: Praeger, 1974.

5 Community Reaction to Bus Mass Transit

The sight of a typical city bus making its rounds is not likely to conjure up the notion of controversy. The viewer may envision such negative aspects of bus transit as long waits, rundown and crowded vehicles, snagged traffic, and high fares, but, typically, community criticism of buses occurs on a small scale and receives little publicity. This chapter addresses a few instances of serious conflict involving bus transit investments and the public.

Investment in bus mass transit systems is subject to quite a different set of issues than need to be considered before investing in the other transportation modes. For instance, the single most controversial aspect of other transportation investments, right-of-way acquisition, is not a factor in the provision of most bus services. Investment in buses, therefore, causes much less physical disruption in the urban environment. Because they are more subtle, less often vocalized, and usually more greatly entwined with other social problems, investment issues are not as well defined for bus systems as they have been for other transportation modes.

Since World War II, transportation investment in the United States, both public and private, has been so overwhelmingly committed to highways and automobiles that most citizens have developed a strong bias against support for any form of public transit. Bus transit in particular has suffered a decline characterized by decreasing ridership and increasing costs, to which the typical administrative response has been to decrease service and raise fares. Until recently, the general belief has been that buses had ceased to be a viable mode of transportation for anyone except the carless and other transportation-disadvantaged persons. Today, bus transit subsidy has become a major transportation issue in many communities. Decisions are being made concerning whether or not to subsidize the buses—and if so, who should do it, how, and to what degree. Many believe the issue has surfaced now because it reflects changing priorities. There is a clear movement away from total commitment to the automobile to a more balanced transportation investment plan. The concept of a subsidy for no-fare bus service has been much debated in transportation literature, especially with respect to its role in promoting a switch from driving one's own car to using mass transit. Another question which arises is whether no-fare or decreased-fare policies would attract enough new riders to warrant the additional expense. A less obvious bus investment question relates to concomitant deficiencies in, or utter lack of, coordinated transit investment policies. Only within the last ten years has the general citizenery begun to be aware of the serious problems faced by persons totally dependent on inadequate bus transit.

The three case histories that follow provide differing examples of community reaction to a number of transportation investment issues. Problems partially resulting from the lack of a coordinated investment plan are described in the case of the 1965 riots in South Central Los Angeles (the Watts area). Community reactions to proposed changes in investment priorities are examined in the case of Houston, where people depend for mobility almost entirely upon cars. The "Magic Carpet Service" of downtown Seattle illustrates the outcome of successful investment in no-fare bus transit.

Watts 1965: Transportation and Poverty

On Wednesday, August 11, 1965, a young black man was arrested for drunken driving on a street in South Central Los Angeles, near the area known as Watts. The young man's arrest drew a large crowd including his mother, whose admonishments angered her son. His anger turned into bitter resentment against the arresting officers. Attempts to control the man culminated in a disruptive scene, at which five people were arrested, including the young man's mother and brother. All of this was witnessed by a crowd of more than a thousand spectators. News of the incident spread quickly, and, almost as rapidly, the scene escalated into the worst riot ever to occur in the United States. It lasted six days and eventually encompassed a 46.5-square-mile area of South Central Los Angeles, where two-thirds of the county's population of 650,000 blacks resided. The events of those six days included alternate periods of tense stalemate and extreme violence–burning, looting, sniper fire, and mass attacks against policemen, firemen, and any whites entering the area. The efforts of the nearly 1,600 members of the Los Angeles Police Department and of the sheriff's office were futile as the riot raged out of control from Wednesday until Saturday. Attempts by local black leaders and national personalities like comedian Dick Gregory were no more successful at quieting the furor. A state of relative calm was produced only after nearly 14,000 National Guard troops were brought in and an 8:00 P.M. curfew imposed. When the curfew was lifted on Tuesday, thirty-four persons had been killed, 1,032 reported injured, and 3,952 arrested. Six hundred buildings were damaged by looting and burning, of which 200 were totally destroyed, with property damage estimated at over $40 million.

The riot was a shock to the nation, even though it had transpired in the shadow of riots the summer before in other cities. It occurred at almost the very moment when civil-rights actions were made a high federal priority– implementation of the Voters' Rights Act, for instance, had begun just that week. Indeed, the Urban League had named Los Angeles the highest-ranking major U.S. city with respect to general conditions in black residential areas.

Immediately after the riot, Governor Edmund Brown appointed an investigatory commission chaired by John A. McCone, former Central Intelligence Agency head and a citizen of Los Angeles.

The commission spent three months hearing testimony from all segments of the community, engaging consultants to study areas of particular concern, and generally investigating sources of unrest. The findings of the McCone commission suggested that the August explosion had its origin in reasons similar to those cited for the riots of the previous summer. They included extremely high unemployment, deficient educational facilities, and serious conflict and distrust between law-enforcement officials and local residents. The McCone report was widely criticized by members of the consulting staff, by other social scientists, and by later studies. Critics deplored the report's analytical selectivity and alleged that the facts had been whitewashed. Significantly, however, one section of the report was widely quoted and its import reinforced by numerous subsequent studies—the section on the relationship of transportation deficiencies to the Watts problems and to poverty and unemployment in general. One passage of the report described the Los Angeles public transportation network as the least adequate of any in the country and recognized that other problems there were only intensified by the transportation deficiency in Watts. The McCone report was the first to recognize that adequate transportation is a significant factor in fighting widespread local unemployment and poverty.

Until August 1965, Watts was little known or generally ignored by the rest of Los Angeles. Most Los Angeles residents believed there were no serious race problems in their city. Even the appearance of the Watts area was deceptive. Unlike eastern ghettos, single-family homes dominated the wide, tree-lined streets. Inside these small homes in a twenty-five-block area, however, were 80,000 people. Watts had the highest population density in the country. Also inside these homes were large numbers of unemployed people—about 30 percent of the residents, as compared to 6 percent in the rest of Los Angeles and the country. The people of Watts and other South Central poverty areas felt cut off from the middle-class blacks on the other side of the Harbor Freeway, where employment was high and life was more prosperous. The inhabitants of Watts could see the general prosperity around them. They could also hear promises of federal assistance, but they saw little evidence of it in their area. Los Angeles was far behind other cities in establishing an effective local antipoverty program. Most social services were housed outside the area; decent hospital facilities were thirty to fifty minutes away. Educational facilities were the most overcrowded in the city, and the dropout rate was high. There were no major sources of employment anywhere in South Central Los Angeles. Residents have no place to take their comments and complaints. What black leadership there was for Watts came from outside the community, belonged to the middle class, and was totally out of touch with the problems in Watts. A fundamental problem for Watts was—and still is—its self-image as a stepping-stone community.

If a resident landed a permanent job, he or she would move to a more comfortable area, away from Watts and its problems. Although there were local political organizations, most were young and somewhat radical and totally without political power. The people were essentially unrepresented. Watts was a power vacuum. To further complicate all of these problems, the transit service was inadequate: very inconvenient and too expensive.

The public transportation system, and the bus service in particular, were grim throughout Los Angeles. The entire area had been served in the past by many private bus companies, most of which were taken over by the Metropolitan Transit Authority in 1958. The MTA was succeeded by the Southern California Rapid Transit District (SCRTD), created by the state legislature in November 1964. The SCRTD, which served Los Angeles County and three adjacent counties with 1,500 buses, was not subsidized at all. Like many other bus systems, the SCRTD had to contend with severe decline, and it treated the problem as other systems had done: it decreased service and increased fares. But Los Angeles was the only major metropolitan area in the country which did not supplement the fare revenue of its bus system in some way.

The SCRTD, two other public companies, and one private company all served the Watts area; each had exclusive rights by law to operate within a given area. Travelers on these assorted buses were given no free transfers, and there was no coordination of routes or schedules. An area resident would often have to ride several buses and pay several fares simply to leave the local area. The long-line transport in and out of Watts and other areas of the city was provided by SCRTD. This service permitted few direct connections and was seriously deficient in cross-town service. Moreover, the SCRTD provided no free transfers between separate urban areas or between its long-line and local bus services. Testimony given by one Watts resident during the postriot investigation underlined the frustrating and often impossible situations encountered by residents without cars. This man testified that in order to reach a job in Santa Monica, about fifteen miles away, he had to change buses four times and spend several hours traveling each way. In addition, he had to pay fares totaling about $3.00 per trip. The transit situation was no worse for Watts than for Los Angeles in general, but it was certainly more critical for Watts, in the light of its many other deficiencies in community services. Statistics vary on car ownership in Watts, but the McCone report estimated that only 14 percent of those living in Watts had cars, as compared with 50 percent for Los Angeles in general. The inadequacy of bus service was particularly crippling to the Watts community, where shopping and medical facilities were seriously lacking, where major sources of employment were nonexistent, and where buses were the only means of transport for the majority of the people.

Many studies, including several presented at the 1968 Conference on Transportation and Poverty, have since been undertaken to study transportation and its relationship to poverty and unemployment. The situation in Watts was an extreme one, but it has been shown time after time that similar conditions exist in cities of all sizes. Poor urban residents, most often members of a minority, are frequently totally dependent on public transportation—that is, they are captive riders and, as such, are transportation-disadvantaged. The highly successful, automobile-oriented transportation of the 1960s rendered many Americans oblivious to the mobility problems of carless people. The findings of the McCone report and of later studies cite the isolation and frustration suffered by members of communities like Watts. All daily activities not within walking distance are hampered by dependence on inadequate bus service. Other studies have pointed out the tremendous advantage car owners have over most public transit riders in making job and housing choices. Considering how massive the social problems of Watts residents had become and how aware of a surrounding prosperity they were, the events of August 1965 seem almost to have been inevitable.

Since the 1965 riots, millions of dollars have been poured into various projects aimed at improving the plight of Watts and other South Central and East Los Angeles poverty areas. Social services have been brought to the people through the establishment of branch offices. Health services have been brought closer by means of new facilities—such as a new hospital and new mental-health and day-care centers. In response to the need for information and guidance about social services, in November 1965 a complaints center was established in Watts using community action funds. Employment services were established by government offices and by the chamber of commerce. For the first time in Watts, a carless person could seek employment without first paying two bus fares and traveling for an hour and a half. Hundreds of action groups were formed by residents seeking self-help solutions.

Efforts were made to solve the transportation problems of the riot area and, to a lesser degree, of the entire Los Angeles system. The Transportation-Employment Project, the largest of such efforts, was begun in 1966 under a $2.7 million grant from the Department of Housing and Urban Development. The initial aim of the project was to increase employment opportunities by providing cross-town bus service to an industrial employment center near the Los Angeles International Airport. That bus service was the first direct convenient means citizens of Watts had of reaching a major source of employment in the greater metropolitan area. The service was a limited success: most of the participants took advantage of the service only until they could save enough money for a down payment on a car.

There were two more phases of the Transportation-Employment Project, one involving studies of the public transit needs of the South Central and East Los Angeles areas, and the other, implementation of study recommendations. As a result of the studies, demand-activated bus service was provided for home-to-work, transit feeder, shopping, medical, and service-center trips.

The Transportation-Employment Project ended in 1971 at a final cost of more than $5 million. It left Watts only marginally better off than it had been in 1965, since no city service replaced HUD's bus lines.

Actual improvements in the Los Angeles public transit system were minimal and slow in coming. The SCRTD continued to be supported by fares at a loss until 1967, when a sales tax rebate was approved to help subsidize transit fares for the elderly and handicapped. In 1971, a statewide permanent rebate on gas sales tax was approved; monies were to be used for transit only and to be channeled to local and county governments. In 1975 the funds for Los Angeles were still being turned over to the SCRTD, which had total transit authority. Nevertheless, because each governmental entity specifies the purpose for which the money is to be spent, the rebate funds have had a minimal effect in Los Angeles. Today, Los Angeles is rated a poor twenty-seventh place, among the twenty-eight major cities, in the provision of mass transit service. Overall conditions in Watts improved in the ten years following the riots, but in terms of bus transit, Los Angeles remains slow to respond to the needs of Watts, in particular, and of the city in general.

Houston: How Much Longer Can the Automobile Reign?

Houston, Texas, is a city of automobiles. It is a sprawling metropolitan region extending into six counties and encompassing more than 6,200 square miles, 506 of which are within the city itself. A young, dynamic, diverse city—a center for petroleum, space programs, sophisticated medical practice and research, and shipping—it was designed and built for automobile users. How easily can the priorities of Houstonians be redirected from freeways to mass transit? To judge from public response to the mass transit referendum of October 1973, much effort and time will be required.

A 1973 Census Bureau study cited Houston among those major metropolitan areas most dependent on cars—87 percent of the work force used cars to get to their jobs. In 1973, only 3 percent used the transit service. In 1972, in Harris County alone, there were nearly 1.3 million cars, the number increasing annually about 7 percent. Within the city proper, there were 300 miles of completed or planned freeway. Even today, a one-way trip of fifty miles is not uncommon for Houston commuters. The city is under considerable pressure from the Environmental Protection Agency to reduce pollution by somehow greatly reducing automobile traffic. Meanwhile, congestion is increasing rapidly. Most citizens favor reductions in pollution and congestion, but most would rather not consider relinquishing their cars in order to achieve those reductions.

Positive acton to explore solutions to the congestion problem and to consider mass transit measures began in October 1970 with an Urban Mass Transit Administration (UMTA) grant to the city Transit Action Program (TAP) to study a balanced public transportation system for the Houston metropolitan area with the city providing one-third of the budgeted $774,000. TAP hired Alan M. Voorhees and Associates, Inc., a well-known transportation consulting firm, to act as program consultants. The concerns and objectives of the study, as outlined by TAP, included working closely with pertinent governments and the public. Attempts were made to accomplish this goal, including wide distribution of a publication called *Newsbriefs*, which informed citizens about the progress of the study. In September 1971, a community advisory committee composed of a hundred citizens was appointed by the mayor to exchange information and opinions with the consultants in a monthly meeting. After twelve months of work, the consultants submitted recommendations to TAP for a $1.45 billion, areawide public transportation plan to be completed in two stages over a period of fifteen years.

The plan called for construction of eighty-one miles of rapid transit conduits, including fixed guideways (most likely rail) and busways (grade-separated roadways) to be reinforced by a restructured and greatly improved bus service. All four of the projected fixed guideway paths would reach a two-mile downtown subway, and the three busways would be built along major freeways in cooperation with the Texas Highway Department. Stage one was to concentrate on the city within Loop 610, and stage two would expand the system to include eventually all of Harris and adjacent counties. People movers, speed walks, and fringe parking areas would be provided as auxiliaries to the main system. The program called for 850 buses, 270 fixed guideway vehicles, and adequate additional maintenance and storage facilities. The report stressed two important points: that continuing support for the local freeway system be maintained and that major improvements in local bus services be provided. The city would have to establish a transit agency to administer the program, and that would first require that enabling legislation be passed on the state level.

In May 1973, the Texas State Legislature passed a bill permitting the Houston City Council to hold public hearings and a referendum for the establishment of a Houston Area Rapid Transit Authority (HARTA). If approved, HARTA would be governed by a board of nine members, appointed by the Houston City Council (five places), the Harris County Commissioners (two places), and the mayors of other cities in the county (two places). Besides granting voter approval of HARTA, the referendum would authorize the board to levy and collect a motor vehicle emission tax. The tax would be based on cubic inches of cylinder displacement, varying from $4 to $15 per year per vehicle.

The Harris County citizens quickly formed two factions. Supporters of HARTA were coordinated by a community improvement committee, headed by former Watergate prosecutor Leon Jaworski. This camp included the mayor and the mayor-elect, the League of Women Voters, the American Association of Architects, the Chamber of Commerce, and a number of other civic and environmental groups. Opposition to HARTA was guided by Sponsors for a

Meaningful Area Rapid Transit (SMART), headed by City Controller Leonel Castillo, a prominent Mexican-American political leader. This camp included the AFL-CIO, the NAACP, the Women's Political Caucus, several Mexican-American civic groups, and most of the suburban mayors.

On October 6, 1973, HARTA and its taxing authority were soundly defeated by a handful of Harris County voters. Only 16 percent of the registered voters came out, but they voted nearly three to one against the referendum. Among blacks, Mexican-Americans, and lower-income whites, the vote was 90 percent against HARTA, as compared with middle-income whites, only 65 percent of whom voted against it.

The proponents had been late in starting their campaign and had failed to draw attention to the positive effects mass transit would have in decreasing congestion. The proposal for HARTA was not necessarily connected to the Voorhees plan, but many believed it was.

Reasons for the defeat were numerous, the primary ones being the tax and the board's proposed authority to levy and collect it without specific voter approval each time. Many believed that the tax would be especially hard on lower-income families, who often owned older cars with larger engines. Others were simply opposed to additional automobile taxes. There were also objections to the lack of a specific plan for areawide mass transit. That was one source of negative votes. Another was the belief that the emission tax would prove insufficient and that additional taxes would be forthcoming. Although citizens had been involved in legislative hearings and had participated in the earlier community adivsory committee, there were still many who argued that citizen participation had been insufficient.

The defeat of the October referendum left Houston-area citizens no better off than they had been in 1970. In fact, several critical issues would have to be faced immediately. A new mayor, Fred Hofheinz, took office in January 1974. He recognized the most immediate problem: the privately owned bus service, Rapid Transit Lines, Inc. (RTL), was losing money and was once again on the verge of increasing fares and decreasing service, primarily because striking bus drivers had forced a promise of higher wages. Immediate action would be necessary to enable the city to purchase the floundering company. The other major problem centered about dissension between government officials and residents over whether the city or the county should take the initiative in establishing a rapid transit authority and over who should control the new agency. City people believed that the county might not act quickly enough to meet their urgent needs, and county people believed they might be left out altogether by the city planners. The situation was further complicated by the fact that the biennial Texas Legislature would not convene again until 1975.

In April 1974, Rapid Transit Lines, Inc., was purchased by the city of Houston for $5.3 million. In addition, the city would pay $250,000 annually for operating expenses. Eighty percent of the purchase price was subsidized by federal funds. A second grant proposal was submitted to the federal government for $4.5 million to purchase 100 new buses. During the following months, the Houston-Galveston Area Council conducted a study on the possibility of paying for an areawide transit service with the help of a grant from UMTA. Hearings concerning mass transit proposals were held in September by both houses of the legislature. In October, the Association of Harris County Mayors and Councilmen voted to develop a proposal for a mass transit system, stressing the need for citizen participation and public hearings to be conducted by the Houston legislative delegation. Meanwhile, city and county officials continued to bicker about whether anything was being done to push forward a mass transit proposal. The mayors' association voted to support a countywide, county-controlled mass transit system which would be funded by state and federal entities, contributions from cities within the county, and contributions from the county.

The newly purchased bus company, renamed HouTran, was expanded to include an additional 563,000 miles of annual service, raising the annual total to 15.9 million miles. The number of buses now totaled 376. The fare for elderly users was reduced from the regular 45¢ to 25¢. The operating deficit for Hou-Tran for 1975 was expected to be $5 million. In December 1974, the city of Houston was designated as the recipient of the $48.6 million appropriated by Congress for mass transit and earmarked for the Houston area, which meant that the city would be the primary recipient and surrounding cities would get a smaller share. Legislative hearings were held in Houston in March 1975 at the county commissioners court regarding amendments to the 1973 bill. Recommendations included (1) prohibiting a transit authority from raising funds without specific voter approval and (2) allowing options for participation by individual cities in the county.

The bill before the Texas legislature in April resurrected the old HARTA but did not empower it to levy taxes without specific voter approval in each case. The membership of the governing board was expanded to admit greater county representation, and provision was made for participation by local option.

Still, complaints were voiced that no specific plan was aligned with the proposal for an areawide mass transit system and the fear was expressed that the city would concentrate on its own problems, ignoring the rest of the county. The local option proposal was another source of dissension. Many felt that participation should be an "all or nothing" affair. In June, the required legislation was passed authorizing a new election for the establishment of a transit authority for Harris County.

During the first year of city ownership, the bus system was gradually improved. In May 1975, the city council approved the Texas Highway Department plan to include a special bus and car-pool lane in the Gulf Freeway expansion project. The lane would extend between Loop 610 and the central business district. Construction was to begin in 1976, with completion expected July

1980. The special lane would be built in the median of the freeway and would accommodate traffic inflow in the morning and outflow in the afternoon. In August, a proposal by Mayor Hofheinz for $21 million worth of improvements to the bus system was endorsed by area businessmen, civic representatives, and governmental agencies. The proposed improvements included 251 new standard-size buses, thirty-seven smaller buses, and twenty vans with special equipment, such as wheelchair lifts, for transporting handicapped and elderly persons. Although there were still no provisions for an areawide system of mass transportation, attempts were being made to improve the existing system, apparently with no adverse reaction from the community. According to local newspapers, opinions regarding transportation needs vary tremendously among Houstonians. Some still believe that cars are the only viable mode and that we should keep building freeways forever, while others argue for expanded bus service, free fares, and bus lanes. Some say buses are not enough and that more advanced modes of transport should be implemented.

In October, 1973, a $1.5 billion proposal for HARTA was defeated by the voters by a margin of 3 to 1. It was to have been funded by an emissions tax based on a complicated formula which was much misunderstood by Houstonians. According to a local transit official, the solution to Houston's problems is still many years away and will probably use the existing freeway system, that is, rapid transit bus service. Other officials maintain that the automobile will always dominate overwhelmingly in the Houston area. The local love affair with the automobile is a deeply rooted relationship. The car represents the freedom to move about, and most mass transit systems, especially the buses, seem to represent limitations. Bus transit is also widely identified with lack of status, crowding, and discomfort. Cars are positively associated with status, privacy, a sense of power, and pleasure. Some Houston officials believe that the number of cars will continue to increase there for many years, though perhaps more slowly than heretofore. It is probable that rising gas prices will eventually force the purchase not of fewer but of smaller cars. An important point to underline with respect to Houston and its acceptance of a mass transit system is that buses (or whatever other mass transport modes are considered) will have to be identified as a means of relieving the problems of air pollution and congestion, not as replacements for the automobile.

Seattle: Magic Carpet Service

Seattle's Metro demonstrates how the elements of active citizen participation, intergovernmental cooperation, and innovative planning can combine to achieve a successful bus service. It is important, in the midst of a discussion of controversies in transportation investment, to stress that a positive approach to solving mass transit problems can be rewarded with a popular and viable bus service.

During the years 1971-1975, Seattle's old bus service was completely revitalized into a system so convenient and attractive that bus manufacturers could not produce new buses fast enough to meet the demand.

Seattle is a city of 550,000 people, but it counts nearly two million in its greater metropolitan area. Lying in a coastal inlet, it is almost totally enclosed by the Olympic and Cascade mountains. In the early 1970s, with its growing number of people and, consequently, of automobiles, Seattle faced serious downtown congestion and even more serious air pollution problems. Because of its geographic location, it could not depend on the wind to disperse the pollution, as some cities have done. Part of the city's approach to solving its problems has been a commitment to improved bus service, and, in the downtown area, to the establishment of a free bus system, the Magic Carpet Service.

Traditionally, Seattle provided its inhabitants with a better than average bus service, but in 1971, the bus service was found inadequate. Much of the equipment was worn out, service was limited, and suburban lines nonexistent. In September 1972, Seattle and surrounding King County approved a levy (of 0.3 percent of the sales tax collected by the state) to support an improved and expanded metropolitan transit service. The Municipality of Metropolitan Seattle (Metro), a federation of all of the governmental entities in the county, was given the authority to administer the program.

Metro had been created in 1957 by state enabling legislation and county voter approval. The functions of Metro were to be overseen by a council of thirty-five members representating all of the entities in the federation. But until 1972, Metro's only functions had been to operate water and waste management facilities, even though the law had provided for its having a more comprehensive role in metropolitan affairs. It had been impressively successful in its first undertaking—to clean up Lake Washington—and had thus earned the respect of the city.

The plan developed for the new transit system included freeway lanes exclusively for buses and new, low-pollution buses. Funding was provided by fares, the general sales tax mentioned above, and state motor vehicle taxes, each supplying about one-third. The new transit arrangement was in operation only a year when the new Magic Carpet Service, Seattle's free downtown bus service, was begun.

Before September 1973, the downtown Seattle area was served by a 10¢ shuttle which brought in $64,000 per year in fares. Urged by Mayor Wes Uhlman, the city tried a one-year experiment with free bus service in the downtown area. The city provided a $64,000 subsidy to Metro to operate the service. Rather than fund a feasibility study which would have cost the same, the city chose to run the experiment itself. There was minimal citizen opposition to the service. A few objected to minor route changes, and taxi drivers mistakenly feared a loss of business. But it was a success. The Magic Carpet Service operates within a 110-block downtown area where the three largest department stores, numerous hotels, small shops, and government offices are located. Buses make 5,400 trips into the downtown area each day, and rides are free in the specified zone. Along with ridership, the popularity of the service has grown steadily from the beginning. Within three months, ridership in the free zone rose 56 percent. In six months, ridership had doubled to 11,000 per day. As a consequence, downtown business has been boosted, and congestion in the area has decreased remarkably. Although no measurements are available, officials believe that pollution and energy consumption have decreased as well.

The expansion and improvement of downtown and areawide services were important to the success of the Magic Carpet Service. Improvements included expanded routes, especially in the suburban areas, park-and-ride lots for downtown express buses, and special buses for transport to outer recreation areas, such as the ski slopes. There were changes in the fare structure. Outside the free zone, fares were lowered to 20¢ in an intermediate zone and 30¢ in an outer zone. Elderly persons were charged a special 10¢ fare. Metro has introduced other fare innovations on the basis of extensive experiments. Monthly transferable passes can be purchased, whose main use is among family members. An annual pass, which is not transferable, can also be bought by heavy users of the Metro. Consumer services have become a significant part of Metro's response to community needs. Signs have been altered to give more information, a central telephone number provides route information, and separate brochures for each route are available on buses and in department stores. In May 1974, awarding a $36.3 million grant to Seattle's bus systems, the Urban Mass Transportation Administration designated Seattle's improvement program the most sophisticated and comprehensive one it had ever financed. The improvements included more park-and-ride lots, express bus stations, new buses, signs, and pollution control devices. The goals of the program are to add three to four million riders per year—up to 54 million by 1980.

Established as a result of citizen concern, Metro continues to be committed to citizen involvement in its decision-making process. Public opinion regarding route changes and schedule adjustments is sought through neighborhood meetings and professionally conducted surveys. The objectives of the Transit Advisory Committee, a group of citizen representatives nominated by each community in the county, include direct participation by as many citizens as possible and provision of a forum for review of transportation needs. Its monthly meetings are always crowded, and citizens are eager to serve on the committee.

The free bus service in Seattle continues to be a success. In September 1974 and again in 1975, the service was extended. Funds were provided by the city of Seattle and, according to some sources, by the local merchants' association as well. The success is attributable to more than just the elimination of fares. Continuing improvements in overall bus service are crucial to the effectiveness of the no-fare service. Elimination of fares cannot take the place of frequent buses and expanded routes.

Citizens have discovered that the bus service is convenient and responsive to their needs. The free downtown service is seen as a bonus. Citizen confidence in Metro and the priority Metro gives to citizen participation keep the system vital. It is the effective combination of many elements in the planning and implementation of innovations that has brought success to Metro and the Magic Carpet Service.

Community Response

The question inevitably arises, why have these communities responded so variously to bus service improvement programs? Differences in attitude and tradition may account for some of the variety. In contrast to the other two cities, Seattle was especially concerned to solve the problem of air pollution; this probably made an enormous difference. While Los Angeles and Houston continue to have high pollution levels, they can depend, partially at least, on the wind to disperse the problem. Because of its geographic situation, Seattle cannot count on that factor and cannot risk an air pollution buildup. Just why Seattle has always wanted to maintain an above-average bus service is unclear, but it is likely that Seattle's decision to implement a top-notch bus service as a partial solution to the problem of air pollution has its origin in Seattle's traditional high regard for buses. Inhabitants of that region of the United States seem to be more concerned with environmental quality. Neither Houston nor Los Angeles has a tradition of good bus service, a fact recently confirmed by the Council of Municipal Research. Of the twenty-eight major U.S. metropolitan areas, Houston rated nineteenth and Los Angeles twenty-seventh in provision of bus service. Both cities were built with automobiles in mind and both remain dedicated to their use, in spite of overwhelming traffic congestion. Both are also situated in states with powerful highway departments. Finally, the way these two cities sprawl does not lend itself easily to the provision of efficient bus service.

A fundamental difference between the three cities in their political organization. Seattle's citizens have confidence in Metro as an efficient intergovernmental operation. The cooperation among its thirty-five member entities and representatives seem exceptional. Houston's political situation provides a strong contrast: the city clashes continually with the county and with other cities in the county. The case of HARTA demonstrates the kind of power struggle that often takes place in Houston. The intergovernmental cooperation which would be necessary to make HARTA work does not seem immanent. Likewise, the various incorporated cities of the Los Angeles Metropolitan area appear to have their own defensively independent attitudes. These, of course, place a barrier against the kind of cooperation necessary to achieve such a goal as an areawide comprehensive bus service. Citizen participation in the decision-making of Seattle's Metro leads to productive communication of a kind sadly absent in Houston and Los Angeles.

No clear answer emerges to explain the different attitudes toward bus service expressed by Watts residents and Houston minorities. Obviously, the 1965 riots in Watts were not merely an expression of a desire for better transit. But the need was clearly there. A few statistics may help to clarify the issue. Whereas 87 percent of the Houston work force depended on cars for work trips, in Los Angeles only 70 percent did. The figures suggest that a greater need for bus service existed in Los Angeles, whether or not the people chose to drive cars. Public reaction to the Transportation-Employment Project demonstrated significantly that Watts residents preferred cars and purchased them as soon as they had the money, instead of continuing to depend on public transit. The overwhelming opposition to HARTA was in part a reflection of the minorities' objection to what they considered an unfair emission tax and to taxes for a poorly designed transit plan. While most of these conclusions are at least partially speculative, they do perhaps shed some light on the contrasting reactions to bus transit in the three cities.

Bibliography

"Black Ghetto in Revolt." *Economist*, 21 August 1965, pp. 692-93.

California Governor's Commission on the Los Angeles Riots. *Violence in the City—An End or a Beginning?* Sacramento, California, 2 December 1965.

Fogelson, Robert M. "White on Black: A Critique of the McCone Commission Report on the Los Angeles Riot." *Political Science Quarterly*, September 1967, pp. 337-67.

"Forgotten Slum." *Nation*, 30 August 1965, p. 89.

Herr, Phillip B., and Fleischer, Aaron. "The Mobility of the Poor." Paper presented at the Transportation and Poverty Conference, June 7, 1968. American Academy of Arts and Sciences, Brookline, Massachusetts.

Kain, John, and Meyer, John. "Transportation and Poverty." *The Public Interest*, Winter 1970.

Kidder, Alice E., and Saltzman, Arthur. *Transportation Problems of the Autoless Worker in a Small City.* Greensboro, North Carolina, 1972.

Kroll, Betty. "Seattle's Transit Triumph: Free Bus Service." *Nation*, 14 September 1974, pp. 210-12.

"Los Angeles: Still Facing Trouble." *U.S. News and World Report*, 15 November 1966, p. 58.

Munro, Donald F., and Krinbring, Brian A. "Seattle Tries Free Downtown Buses." *Civil Engineering—ASCE*, August 1974, pp. 86-87.

News Releases by the Houston Transit Action Program.

Newsletters of the Texas Good Roads/Transportation Association.

Ognibene, P.J. "Free Ride." *New Republic*, 16 March 1974, pp. 10-11.

Ornati, Oscar A. *Transportation Needs of the Poor*. New York: Praeger, 1969.

Rosenbloom, S. "The Social Benefits of the Proposed Multi-Service Transportation (MUST) Systems in East Los Angeles and South Central Los Angeles." Transportation-Employment Project of the State of California, Sacramento, November 1969.

"Seattle Receives Grant to Expand Bus System." *Wall Street Journal*, 7 May 1974.

"Seattle's Free Buses Revitalize Downtown Area; They Save Gas, But Traffic, and Spread Goodwill." *Wall Street Journal*, 12 February 1974.

Houston Chronicle and *Houston Post*, 1973-75, various articles.

Los Angeles Times, various articles.

New York Times, various articles from 1965 and 1966 issues.

"Watts Revisited." *Economist*, 13 August 1966, p. 645.

Weise, Arthur E. "Houston: High Hopes for Mass Transit." *Mass Transit*, October 1974, p. 17.

"Why Houston Voters Vetoed Mass Transit." *Business Week*, 13 October 1973, p. 28.

Part II: Theory

Philosophical and Economic Issues

Adverse public reaction to urban transport proposals results from problems caused, at least in part, by inadequate government planning. Public administrators have not been sufficiently cognizant of negative sociological, environmental, and economic effects a project may have. As a result of poor planning, roads have divided neighborhoods, parks have been ruined, and whole areas have stagnated. A list of specific problems would seem endless. Economists have been formulating decision standards and project selection procedures in an attempt to upgrade the quality of policy decisions. Their efforts have developed a philosophy of decision-making related to improving public welfare. In practice, these philosophies have been translated into various forms of benefit-cost analysis, procedures primarily concerned with the investment decision. Short-run capacity problems involve, on the other hand, the use of the existing supply of transportation services. New highways, airports, and railroads take time to build. That is why consumer demands for transportation services must be met, at least temporarily, with existing facilities. If demands are not satisfied quickly, public reaction may be negative. I discuss these issues in the following sections.

The Philosophy of Public Decisions

The promotion of public well-being is the foundation of welfare economics. In order to advance public welfare, an economist must be capable of determining which policy changes will mean improvements. If he cannot, the economist is in no position to make any recommendations at all.

Seeking to facilitate the making of sound policy judgments, economists—for the past fifty or so years—have been developing welfare decision standards to perfect universally adaptable criteria for the advancement of public welfare. Unfortunately, the criteria for welfare judgment have tended to be too global and abstract to be of much use to decision-makers. The decision standards are important because they provide decision-makers with normative bases for judgment. In other words, welfare judgment criteria are relevant because decision-makers are told what *should* occur in the best of circumstances.

Many appraisals of public well-being can be made by decision-makers without the aid of judgment criteria. For instance, in earlier periods of development in the United States, public desire for transportation facilities was obvious. During the Great Depression, reduction of unemployment was an apparent social need. In such cases, decision-makers needed no formal criteria for welfare judgment to appraise the need for expanded facilities or increased employment. The needs of the society were obvious—at least to the great majority.

Today, exhaustive assessment criteria are needed to evaluate projects where improvement in the common well-being is not so obvious. The urban transportation projects of the present and the future are just the type of projects needing that sort of critical assessment. Freeway projects, airport proposals, and rail transportation projects must all be individually and jointly appraised by some normative criterion. After initial evaluation, decision-makers can consider the individual singularities of projects.

Nearly every change affects some people favorably and other people adversely. Usually there is no satisfactory means of quantifying the net effect of a project on society. Nevertheless, policymakers must make decisions on a case-by-case basis. Highway agencies and railroad commissions must make interpersonal comparisons for each project. For instance, in Austin the Texas Highway Department determined that the MoPac Expressway would advance the general public well-being even though it would disturb many people along its path. Still, no formula has been invented which can judge every case equitably.

Policymakers should attempt, perhaps, to use the general formulations of welfare judgment theory as a basis for decisions, aware though they be of the inadequacies of these formulations. At the very least, policymakers should attempt to estimate the extent of damage possible under each proposal. Virtually every project harms some people. If enough people are harmed or if those harmed are powerful enough, they may enter the political process and attempt to stop project construction. This is exactly what happened in the MoPac Expressway controversy. The people harmed by the expressway's traffic were relatively rich and powerful people. They used their influence on the Austin city council. Although their efforts were not successful, their endeavors exemplify the way people will enter the political process in an attempt to halt project completion. Clearly, to avoid wasteful conflict, policymakers must attempt to measure the extent and distribution of proposed welfare improvements and then use that information in making publicly acceptable decisions.

At attempt to develop a generally applicable welfare judgment criterion was developed by Vilfredo Pareto, an Italian economist. He defined an *improvement* as any change that injures no one but ameliorates conditions for others to the extent that they are aware of the change for the better. The Pareto criterion is not applicable in the vast majority of cases, since nearly every project harms someone. In the estimation of the injured, virtually no project would be considered an improvement. Certainly none of the projects presented in this book could be considered optimal according to the Pareto criterion. For instance, the Bay Area Rapid Transit system was objectionable to some groups of people because they believed the system to be harmful to the environment in which they lived. Another example could be the Los Angeles Airport project, which displaced many citizens. Those injuries were aggravated by increases in the airport's noise. Under the Pareto criterion, few projects would qualify.

Nonetheless, the Pareto criterion is potentially helpful because it can serve as a normative basis for judgment and be used to describe the optimal benefits of a welfare project. Pareto optimality would result when a change would benefit some people without having any deleterious effects. This would allow a number of projects under consideration to be assessed relative to the Pareto optimal situation and ranked. Unfortunately, the evaluation of Pareto optimality involves a number of complications, the worst of which is that citizen preferences must be accurately measured for this determination to be valid. The difficulty, of course, would tend to constrain policymakers in their attempt to measure Pareto optimality.

Another criterion for welfare judgment was developed by Nicholas Kaldor in the 1940s. Kaldor defined a change as an improvement if those who gain feel more strongly that they *have* gained than those harmed feel they have been harmed. Kaldor argued that if the gainers in a change could compensate the injured for their losses and yet manage to keep a part of the gain for themselves, then the change would be an improvement. No redistribution of wealth is necessary for the Kaldor criterion to hold. The only requirement is that the gainers be capable of compensating the losers. Once the compensation has been made, theoretically the improvement would meet the Pareto criterion.

A major inadequacy of the Kaldor criterion is that it only relates to efficiency considerations and does not relate to equity considerations. A project may have redistribution effects and pass the Kaldor test with flying colors. The Watts neighborhood case provides a good example here. A freeway built near the Watts area passes the Kaldor test because the users of the freeway gained more than the poor people in Watts lost. The poor people lose because they have to endure the freeway *and* its bad effects–noise, air pollution, ugliness, and neighborhood disruption. Because no compensation is required for the Kaldor criterion to be valid, judgments made using it may not be fair to all groups concerned.

Yet another welfare judgment criterion has been developed by Paul Samuelson. He has stated that a project should be accepted if wealth distribution is made no worse by the project, the externalities sum to zero, and no mutually exclusive better option is available. When the acceptance of one option precludes the selection of any other choice which might have been considered, the option is said to be mutually exclusive. Samuelson requires that the best of all mutually exclusive options be selected. For example, to meet Samuelson's standard, highway departments should investigate *all* highway routes available before choosing the best of the (mutually exclusive) route alternatives. Samuelson requires decision-makers to determine the wealth distribution effects of a project: no project should be accepted if it is inequitable. Externalities–the extra, non-intentional effects that a project may have (air pollution, for example)– should sum to zero. Such side effects may be beneficial or costly to society. Samuelson believes that, for a project to be accepted, beneficial and costly externalities should at least balance each other. Otherwise, the project might prove potentially harmful. Samuelson's three requirements provide administrators with a concrete basis for making welfare judgments and are particularly applicable in the consideration of transport project proposals.

Henri Bergson, the French philosopher, believed that the only way to decide if a project will result in an improvement is to formulate a set of specific value judgments against which the analyst can evaluate proposed changes. The value judgments—on what constitutes justice, equity, and virtue—can be drawn up by an economist, a legislative body, or any other group or person entrusted with the task of assessing society's preferences. Unfortunately, Bergson provided no way to formulate the explicit value judgments into a model. His criterion, therefore, is not especially useful to decision-makers.

Another welfare judgment criterion has been developed by Kenneth Arrow, on the basis of the way democratic groups make decisions. The minimal conditions that group choices must meet in order to reflect individual preferences are four. First, the group's choice among current alternatives must be confined to, and reflect, public preferences among those alternatives which are indeed current. Second, no one outside the community affected should be allowed to dictate decisions. Third, choices must be consistent. If one project is preferred to a second and the second preferred to a third, the third must not be chosen above the first. Fourth, group decisions must reflect the direction of citizen preferences. Arrow was concerned with the problem of combining individual preferences into a reasonable group decision that would reflect accurately individual desires within the group. But, using sophisticated mathematical techniques, Arrow has demonstrated that group decisions *must* violate at least one of the stated minimal conditions. The implication of his work is that group decisions must necessarily be undemocratic.

In most cases, the measurement of welfare improvements on a national scale is beyond our current abilities. The elements of social welfare cannot be determined fairly for the entire society. It has been argued that a decision-maker should, as a practical matter, concentrate on local welfare improvements, since our inability to measure the preferences of society at large makes national welfare optimization difficult, if not impossible. Furthermore, the relation between local improvements and national improvements is not known, and that information is needed before decisions based on the social welfare of the entire society can be made. If the social sciences develop to the point where the preferences of society can be effectively measured, the policymaker would then be able to make global decisions. At this time, however, it seems wiser for policymakers to concentrate on local rather than goal improvements.

Benefit-Cost Decision Analysis

Benefit-cost decision analysis is designed to evaluate objectively a project's merits. The purpose of the procedure is to improve allocation of public resources. Several different variations of benefit-cost analysis have in the past been used. Examples are the benefit-cost ratio, present worth, internal rate of return, and benefits minus costs. Computation of the benefit-cost ratio is the method most widely used in government circles. Decision analysis is conducted by:

1. defining and weighting objectives by their perceived importance,
2. identifying all alternatives,
3. predicting and estimating all beneficial and costly consequences, and
4. making a decision.

Benefits and costs can only be measured with respect to an objective. Theoretically, they can be calculated for any desired objective. The profit motive serves as the private sector's basic objective, although other things, such as good labor relations, may also occasionally serve. In the public sector, the objective should be unambiguous improvement of the social welfare. Decision-makers should make every attempt to achieve that objective by trying to measure the relative value of a broad range of desired objectives. For example, a government administrator may decide from a citizen hearing that the public desires a faster route to work, more park and recreation areas, reduced pollution, safer transportation, and no visible structures. The administrator must formulate objectives from these desires. Then, he should determine the relative importance society places upon each desire. Unfortunately, this is a complicated task. Society's preferences can be defined by legislators, governmental agencies, ballot boxes, statistical samples, or a number of other means. Democratic group choice is probably one of the better procedures; but, as Kenneth Arrow's analysis demonstrated, the choices made may not actually reflect the individual preferences of the group's members. Indeed, all methods of preference measurement provide questionable results. However, no better techniques have been devised than the ones outlined above. Consequently, administrators must use procedures which are currently available to determine the proper weights to place upon objectives. For instance, public officials may decide after a sample has been taken that a ten-acre park saved is equal to 2,000 man-hours saved, and that ten fewer accidents per year is equal to 1,000 man-hours saved. Finally, officials can value the average man-hour at a given monetary rate so that objectives can be weighted. Undeniably such a procedure may admit biases and inaccuracies, but the absence of some sort of explicit weighting system may result in important objectives not being considered at all. An explicit weighting scheme may also ignore some relevant objectives, although it is less likely to do so. The decision as to which objectives are important will always be debatable with regard to any project proposal. That alone will account for many of the differences in the application of benefit-cost analysis.

Identification of the various alternatives available should follow the specification of objectives. All alternatives need to be technically possible and within the proposed project budget. Furthermore, alternatives should be mutually exclusive; that is, the selection of one should preclude the selection of all others. Alternatives cannot be dependent on each other.

Each alternative must satisfy at least one objective. It is not necessary to satisfy all possible objectives with every alternative. An alternative might be selected if it satisfies a few objectives well, even though other objectives are not achieved by it. If all alternatives that satisfy even one objective are included, the decision-maker will have a broad range of choices at his disposal.

Preserving the existing situation is always an alternative. It provides at least two choices, to build or not to build. Following existing policies and making no changes is frequently the best alternative to take. Usually it is chosen when negative effects of a proposed project overwhelmingly stack up against some important objective.

Determining and assessing benefits and costs for each alternative is the next step in the analysis. Benefits are measures of the effectiveness of a project in achieving a desired objective. Costs are measures of the resources sacrificed to achieve the desired objective.

Direct costs include investment, maintenance, and operation expenses. These can be measured in monetary terms. Other, more indirect, costs cannot be measured precisely in monetary terms. Examples of indirect costs are increased pollution and destruction of park lands. It is difficult to assess the value of such sacrifices. Some benefits may also be difficult to quantify in dollar terms. An indirect benefit might be reduced street traffic resulting from construction of a new road. *Indirect consequences* is another name for externalities.

Benefits and costs must be weighted by their incidence in time: will the consequences occur immediately, in the near future, or in the distant future? Consequences have a time value. This means that people would rather have the pleasant happen sooner, the unpleasant later. The concept is applied by using a percentage discount rate. The purpose of the rate is to value benefits and costs occurring in the future at the value society places on them in the present.

The selection of a discount rate involves a value judgment. A higher rate will make future consequences less important by valuing their benefits or costs at a smaller present figure. The choice of a lower rate has the opposite effect. Decision-makers must select a discount rate that accurately represents society's time valuation.

After the benefits and costs of each alternative are compared, a decision is made. Comparisons are made by dividing discounted benefits by discounted costs, by subtracting costs from benefits, or by some other method. A project is said to be acceptable if the total benefits exceed the total costs. All other things remaining equal, the project scoring the highest positive value is selected.

Benefit-cost analysis methods vary from analyst to analyst because several value judgments must be made to implement the analysis. Objectives must be defined; this involves value judgments. In the past, many civil engineers refused to consider any objective except the maximization of directly quantifiable user benefits over costs. The engineers' reasoning was that since all other objectives must be estimated by inaccurate methods, the best objective is the one accurately quantifiable. Other analysts believe project objectives should be expanded to include all of society's preferences. Their reasoning is that all preferences should be included, whether this can be done accurately or not, because these other preferences are as relevant as monetary costs.

Determination of the relevant benefits and costs also involves value judgments. Traditional engineers still believe that only quantifiable direct consequences should enter policy determinations. Others believe the indirect consequences to be just as important as the direct ones. Consequently, the latter group always includes estimates of indirect consequences in their analyses.

The choice of the discount rate also involves assumptions. Some theorists believe a low rate represents society's time preference; others hold that a higher rate is more representative.

All of these value judgments have resulted in the use of several different kinds of benefit-cost analysis. Theoretically, the expanded versions should give better results. Practically, the estimation problems complicate the determination of the validity of each analysis.

Two economists, Martin McGuire and Harvey Garn, have developed a benefit-cost analysis which combines qualitative and quantitative judgments into an operational context. Their decision analysis explicitly treats the tradeoff between equity and economic efficiency by mathematically formulating a welfare equity index. The index reflects the economists' assessment of society's preferences for income distribution. Preferences may indicate a redistribution of benefits to the poor. Or a society may wish to make no changes in the income distribution. The McGuire-Garn type of analysis quantifies these preferences. The index is used to weight benefit-cost ratios. Projects can then be selected by a maximum weighted benefit criterion.

Benefit-cost analysis has been discussed here because it is the method of project evaluation used most widely in U.S. cities. Since decisions are being made with this sort of analysis, citizens concerned with or involved in the decision-making process should understand the procedure.

Theoretically, a complete benefit-cost analysis model will furnish the decision which will yield an unambiguous improvement of public welfare.

Problems of definition and quantification make a perfect theoretical model impossible at this time. A complete model, accurate or not, would undoubtedly result in better decisions. The reader should note that in some instances decision-makers may manipulate figures and ignore objectives for reasons other than economic efficiency or equity. But these problems are often discernible in the analysis. Fortunately, benefit-cost analysis forces decision-makers to justify projects with objective data.

Externalities

Externalities, frequently referred to as side effects, indirect consequences, or extramarket effects, are defined simply as divergences between social and private returns. In other words, public and private effects do not coincide. With respect to transportation projects, external costs are such unintentional consequences as destroyed park land, increased pollution, displacement of populations, divided neighborhoods, and increased traffic accidents.

That policymakers should investigate externalities is important, because externalities are often the major causes of conflict, by having an adverse effect on society or on some group within society. Injured citizen groups seek redress through the political process, since compensation for losses is not provided by current economics.

Externalities can be translated into direct consequences. The problem of traffic congestion will be used extensively to exemplify the procedure for placing money values on externalities. In fact, as this example shows, conflict can be reduced merely by pricing the externalities involved.

Externalities have been present in every case presented in this book; indeed, much of the controversy arising in these cases has been caused by externalities. Nearly every transportation project has its externalities, but the cases in this study are particularly important because they represent instances wherein groups are harmed enough to engage in active political conflict.

Citizen groups objected to the construction of a freeway in Memphis's Overton area because it would cut through a park. The destruction of the park is an external cost. The people had to enter the political system because the economic market offered no remedy for their loss.

The BART heavy rail system of San Francisco had some important externalities. A favorable one was the reduction of traffic on roads in the Bay area. Negative effects included the destruction of green areas.

Externalities were present in the Watts neighborhood case, where freeways were built instead of mass transit systems. The indirect effect of that decision was the social isolation of the Watts area. The high cost of individual transportation forced the poor to stay in Watts. They could not afford to travel to jobs outside the area. Eventually the people rioted, and that, too, was an external cost of building freeways rather than low-fare mass transit.

In the case of the Los Angeles Airport, citizens were primarily concerned with the externality of noise pollution. Citizens protested the ugliness of the MoPac Expressway. These cases exemplify the political significance of externalities to construction projects.

For purposes of responsible decision-making, externalities should be transformed into market items when possible. A market item is something which can be purchased in a competitive system. A pricing system for intangible side effects would enable public officials to control some of the problems associated with them. How externalities can be transformed into market items is best described by the example of traffic congestion.

Traffic congestion is defined as a situation where the increased level of usage of an existing transportation facility makes the social costs (costs accruing to everybody) of the additional users exceed the individual private costs incurred by all users. For example, in the case of freeways the user costs are time, car maintenance, gas, oil, and a few other minor expenses. Unfortunately, if too many users get on a freeway at the same time—if congestion occurs—the supernumerary users place an extra cost of time and trouble on everybody. The extra cost is an externality.

Traffic congestion can be priced. Since crowded conditions on freeways—along with the related noise, air, and aesthetic pollution—are a cause of conflict, it would be desirable to make traffic congestion a market item. This would result in a more economical use of existing freeway facilities.

It is the morning and evening rush hours which cause the most severe congestion problems. This is the time when people are going to and from work. Higher prices should be charged during rush hours when rationing is most needed. During slack hours, no price would need to be charged.

Congestion prices would make accessibility a market item instead of an item paid for in extra travel time and trouble. People in a hurry to get to work could pay the charge and take the faster route. People going shopping or driving out for recreation could take a slower route or make a later departure and not have to pay the charge. The congestion price would give the consumer a real choice, and the absence of congestion would become a service to be purchased if desired.

Some economists have objected to the idea of pricing congestion because of the difficulties of quantifying the externalities, a task which must be accomplished to establish an appropriate toll. The objection is not valid. Progress has been made in developing methods of quantifying at least some of the externalities of congestion. The value of extra time has been estimated and related to congestion. Furthermore, if the number of cars is reduced, the nonmarketable externalities of congestion—such as tension, ulcers, and pollution—will also be reduced. They will be reduced merely by a reduction in activity. So, if externalities that can be priced are charged for, then other nonmarketable externalities will also be reduced.

Other important externalities of the congestion-time transit charge would of course include its indirect effects on the infrastructure. The spatial distribution of stores, factories, houses, apartments, schools, and other economic, social, and residential facilities would be affected. Land values and development would be influenced. The spatial distribution of economic classes would be altered. In general, the congestion price would cause a reallocation of resources because of a change in the market value of uncongested traffic. However, the value and extent of these changes are difficult to measure. It is even difficult to describe the changes. But the difficulty should not deter a policymaker from attempting to determine whether or not the congestion price would have adverse effects on some groups.

Criticism has been directed at the congestion-time transit charge because it could redistribute wealth in an undesirable manner. The congestion charge necessary to achieve efficiency during rush hours would probably result in tolls substantially higher than the lower-income individuals could afford. One researcher has estimated that two to three dollars would have to be charged to ration traffic efficiently during rush hours on the average urban freeway. Many people have objected to charging these high prices on the grounds that the toll would force low-income individuals off the road to benefit high-income individuals. Since the value of time generally increases with wealth, the wealthy people would gain more by paying the toll. Furthermore, they can afford to pay it.

Whenever a plan is developed, compensation policies should be established by policymakers to internalize externalities such as road congestion. In the case of the preceding paragraph, revenue collected in the form of a congestion-time transit charge could be used as a subsidy and given to the poor for the use of taxis, buses, or trains. The toll would reduce congestion and at the same time have less of a regressive effect. The poor highway commuter could simply be given a monthly toll rebate. General economic policies such as the progressive income tax are designed to alleviate some of the inequities in the economic system. While these general policies would not eliminate the equity problems of the congestion toll, they do make the equity problems less severe.

Externalities are relevant. They represent a significant portion of the consequences of most projects. They cause conflict between people and policymakers. The pricing of these indirect consequences of changes will result in better utilization of transportation services. People will be able to purchase services and contend with fewer externalities if they so desire. If indirect consequences of projects—or even of existing conditions—are not priced, control over them may be permanently lost to society. To wit, time lost in traffic congestion is lost forever, but if a congestion price is imposed, people can choose not to lose time by paying the charge.

Conflict also can be reduced by pricing externalities. A compensation system often results in reduction of conflict. People who will benefit from a given change can avoid the opposition to the change by paying a price. Compensated, the injured may not seek remedies through conflict—in politics or the courts.

Additional Supply and Demand Considerations

Demand is the fundamental determinant of transportation route location. The supply of facilities is a response to the demand. The demand for transportation projects is generated by the desires of people to move from place to place. People demand transportation facilities for many reasons, but the most significant determinant of demand is the location of jobs. People demand facilities for the journey to work, for the movement of goods, and for shopping and leisure activities.

The short-run solutions to urban transportation problems require satisfying user demands with the existing supply of highways, railroads, and airports. They involve maximizing the efficiency of existing transit systems. If a project satisfies user demands and if the project is built with the least sacrifice necessary, then it is said to be economically efficient. The principal tools for achieving this kind of economic efficiency are tolls, laws, physical barriers, taxes, and subsidies. Tolls can be charged during peak rush hours to ration traffic on the facility. Laws can be passed to regulate speeds and movement. Physical barriers—such as freeway ramp entrance barriers—can be used to regulate the flow of traffic. Gasoline taxes can be levied to discourage the use of automobiles. Subsidies can be provided to underutilized facilities so that their excess capacity will be used to alleviate crowded conditions on other modes of transport. All of these methods can be employed to enhance the efficient use of existing facilities. Often, additional investment in transport facilities would not be needed if existing facilities were priced, or rationed, efficiently.

On the other hand, serious congestion may result from the underprovision of network capacity. Consequently, demand analysis is needed to avoid errors in computing the capacity required. When rationing the use of one facility, provisions should be made for other modes of transit to absorb all of the diverted traffic. Demand analysis should seek to incorporate in its calculations figures for projected, diverted, and newly generated traffic.

Citizens will complain if these needs are not met. Network systems which fail to satisfy the desires of the community efficiently will not be acceptable to the public. Transportation policies must deal with present situations and future proposals. Resources committed to future development cannot be consumed thoughtlessly in the present. Policymakers must make timing decisions. And all of this should be done according to community demands.

Philosophy and Economics Vis-à-vis Conflict:
The Conclusion

The philosophical and economic issues raised in this chapter all relate in critical ways to various philosophies of public decision-making. They provide a basis for formulating opinions on the standards a project must meet to be acceptable.

Students of public decision-making philosophy can consider what elements are necessary to regard a change as an improvement. Benefit-cost analysis, to the extent that it works, is a practical application of the philosophy of decisions. Accordingly, the various value judgments necessary to benefit-cost analysis can be ranked against a standard measure of public advancement. Externalities related to transit changes present both ethical and financial problems, and so may prove the central issues in transportation-related conflicts. Some of the economic problems, of course, are associated with questions of efficiency— how can demands best be satisfied once the supply of transportation services already exists? These problems can be addressed as questions of supply and demand, so long as decision-makers recognize their ethical and financial responsibilities.

The philosophy of government planning and related decision-making models are concerned with satisfying social demands in the best way. This is not to say that everyone affected will be pleased. But when externalities are ignored in the planning stages of transportation projects, even more conflict results because the group that suffers the effects is doubly injured, once by the effect itself, and once more because measures that might have been taken to mitigate the external costs were not employed because they were unforseen. In short, no compensation was provided.

Someone is almost always bound to be hurt by urban mass transit projects. The point is that those who suffer should be compensated.

Bibliography

Ackley, Gardner, *Macroeconomic Theory*. New York: Macmillan, 1970.
*Action Plan for Improvement in Transportation Systems in Large U.S. Metro-
    politan Areas: Auto-Free Zones: A Methodology for Their Planning
    and Implementation*. Washington, D.C.: Barton-Aschman Associates,
    Inc. 1972.
Arrow, Kenneth J. *Social Choices and Individual Values*. Cowles Commission
    Monograph No. 12, New York: John Wiley & Sons, Inc., 1951.
Baumol, William J. *Economic Theory and Operations Analysis*, Third Edition.
    Englewood Cliffs, N.J.: Prentice-Hall, Inc., 1972.
Boulding, Kenneth E., and Pfaff, Martin. *Redistribution to the Rich and the
    Poor*. Belmont, Cal.: Wadsworth Publishing Co., 1972.
Hay, Alan. *Transport for the Space Economy: A Geographical Study*.
    London: Macmillan, 1973.
James, L. Douglas, and Lee, Robert R. *Economics of Water Resources Planning*.
    New York: McGraw-Hill, 1971.
Lansing, John B., and Hendricks, Gary. *Automobile Ownership and Residential
    Density*. Ann Arbor: Institute for Social Research, University of Michigan,
    1970.

Lloyd, Peter R., and Dicken, Peter. *Location in Space: A Theoretical Approach to Economic Geography*. New York: Harper & Row, 1972.

Mishan, E.J. *Cost Benefit Analysis: An Introduction*. New York: Praeger, 1971.

McGillivray, Robert G. *On Road Congestion Theory*. Washington, D.C., The Urban Institute, March 1974.

McGuire, Martin C., and Garn, Harvey A., "The Integration of Equity and Efficiency Criteria in Public Project Selection." *The Economic Journal*, December 1969.

Pigou, A.C. *The Economics of Welfare*. Fourth Edition. London: Macmillan, 1932.

Samuelson, Paul A. *Public Economics*. New York: Macmillan-St. Martins, 1969.

Schreiber, Arthur F.; Gatons, Paul K.; and Clemmer, Richard B. *Economics of Urban Problems: An Introduction*. Boston: Houghton Mifflin Co., 1971.

7 Environmental Aspects

The effects of mass transportation systems on the environment go far beyond the various sorts of pollution that have captured so many headlines in the last decade. As the cases in this book illustrate, environmental issues have produced controversy over the construction of ugly freeways, noise pollution, and the destruction of parks and historically significant structures. While other effects— on land use and climate, for instance—are less obvious and thus rarely considered, they are still of considerable long-range importance.

Environmental effects of transportation systems are not necessarily bad, although detrimental effects naturally attract the most attention. Proper understanding of these effects which accompany the different transportation methods will provide additional information about the value of alternative systems and thus should be valuable for planning additions to or alterations in community transportation facilities. Furthermore, a proper understanding of a specific mode's likely effect on the environment will allow the mode's positive aspects to be enhanced fully and enable planners to compensate for negative effects.

Environmental effects occur on several levels and are here considered under four rubrics: immediate sensory effects (such as noise, ugliness, and atmospheric pollution), destruction of valuable properties, effects on land-use patterns, and other effects.

Immediate Sensory Effects

All forms of transit require permanent structures for their operation. These are often highly visible, and all too often do not blend with their surroundings. They are, therefore, one of the most common sources of complaints by citizens who oppose the construction of new transportation systems. The San Francisco Embarcadero Freeway cases provides an outstanding illustration. It was felt to be so ugly and so out of place with its surroundings—the waterfront district of San Francisco—that citizen outrage prevented its completion and forced San Francisco to install the BART rapid rail transit system instead. As the case in chapter four shows, even BART met opposition, on similar grounds, and one community, Berkeley, was willing to foot the bill to put the system underground rather than have it adversely affect their environment.

Roads and rail lines become visible failures in two ways. One way results from the poor design of bridges and viaducts. The other, from a misplaced right-of-way, which often involves not only the location of land to be used for the facility, but also whether or not the road is to be elevated. The Embarcadero Freeway again provides a good example. It was an elevated, double-decked expressway, over two stories high, in an area where most of the surrounding buildings were only two stories high themselves. In addition, its path cut a broad swath through a historic portion of San Francisco, and its placement destroyed the visual effect of a number of fine old buildings, especially the Ferry Building.

Bridges and viaducts have historically produced the best—and the worst—visual effects of transportation structures. Suspension bridges such as the Golden Gate Bridge are beautiful in their own right. Often, however, bridges and viaducts have been poorly designed, overbuilt, and too massive to blend with their environment.

In general, the smaller and lighter the materials used in a structure, the better it blends with its surroundings. Specifically, the superstructure should be minimal, preferably just a deck for the road or rail bed. The supports should be widely spaced and designed to minimize the bulky, blocky effects of the structure. Ornate designs should be omitted, since they serve primarily to emphasize bulk. Current materials technology allows for the construction of longer spans using thinner members, without requiring a superstructure. T-shaped supports further reduce the profile of a bridge by eliminating the need for a row of supports resembling a fishing pier out of water and allowing for a more contoured structure.

In general, misplacement is said to occur when a road, or track, is so designed that it obscures or stands out from the surrounding buildings or land, when a right-of-way fails to follow the contours of its environment, either natural or man-made, or when routes pass through or near areas not visually compatible with the system.

Some of the most poorly designed roads and tracks are elevated structures which, due to their great lengths, loom starkly about their environment. They obscure the original environment instead of blending with it. Misplaced billboards and poorly directed lighting to illuminate highways at night are other offenders. Wide area lighting causes unnecessary illumination of surrounding neighborhoods.

It is because of the safety consideration generally that the problems of wide area lighting and unsightly road elevation arise. Good, safe design requires that roads used at high speeds must be straightened and flattened for improved visibility and control. Highway and railway systems are often forced to elevate to meet required safety standards because previous development of the urban environment, coupled with the natural contours of the land, severely restricts acceptable alternate routes through town. Urban freeways also require more intense lighting, due to heavier traffic and numerous interchanges. However, properly directed and shielded lights can prevent irritating illumination of surrounding neighborhoods.

Another common problem occurs when rights-of-way are not designed to follow the contours of the environment. In highly developed sections, particularly in the central portions of a city, rights-of-way which do not follow existing neighborhood street patterns create wide scars through the areas they penetrate, separating otherwise well-integrated neighborhoods and creating physical and psychological barriers between the divided portions.

The shortest path is not always the best path. In an urban system, it rarely is. Admittedly, it is a difficult task to plan a route through a populated area so as to minimize neighborhood disruption. Failure to plan, however, will often result in controversy which may stop the project halfway or enormously increase its cost. Route planning must take into account the space that transportation structures, especially freeways, require and the effect of those structures on the visual environment.

In areas where rights-of-way pass through or around hills or mountainsides, positioning of the roadbed where cuts and fills will be minimized and careful grading of the cuts where they are necessary will reduce the steplike effect cuts often create. In addition, freeways can be built on two levels—with relatively minor cuts for each direction of traffic, rather than the massive cut and fill necessary for keeping the two halves of a multilane freeway on a common level. Separate roadbeds also minimize grading necessary to achieve good contours.

Safety considerations limit the ability of highway planners to plan a route along existing environmental patterns. Many cities, for instance, have developed from a number of separate cores which merged eventually into a single large metropolitan area. Resulting street patterns tend to be nonuniform, and a freeway built to follow them would have to zig-zag elaborately. As freeway speeds increase, however, planners must strive to straighten the freeway to meet minimum standards of visibility and vehicle control. And the same is true of rail systems. Thus, to a certain extent, disruption of neighborhoods is inevitable. Perhaps because they know this, planners have not always considered alternatives carefully enough and have not, therefore, consistently achieved the best compromises.

Unpleasant sounds and vibrations are persisting problems associated with mass transportation systems. Truck noises, vibrations from rail systems, the roar of jets on takeoff have all sparked their share of public controversy. For roads and rail systems, screens and baffles can reduce levels of noise and vibration. Airports present a more complex problem since jets on takeoff quickly rise above even the most effective screens or baffles that can be constructed.

Freeways used by trucks as well as by vehicles which move people create a noise problem. A truck traveling at 50 mph generates a sound level of ninety-six to ninety-eight Perceived Noise in Decibels (PNDb) at a distance of fifty feet.

By contrast, a living room with people engaged in normal conversation generates a level of about fifty PNDb. Tests on cars to be used in the BART system indicated that they would generate ninety-one to ninety-four PNDb at 55 mph within a range of 150 feet, and a Boeing 707 (1970), two hundred feet in the air after takeoff, generates 100 PNDb to a distance of 2,000 feet on either side. Prolonged high levels of that kind of noise can have a number of detrimental effects on people; it can cause deafness and loss of sleep, with accompanying increases in such nervous disorders as irritability and anxiety.

The problem of vibration, which is particularly of concern in rail-borne systems, can be alleviated to a large extent by using vibration-dampening materials beneath the track so that vibration is not transferred to the supporting structure and thence into the ground. The BART system uses a number of vibration and noise reducing devices, including vibration absorptive pads beneath the rails and acoustically absorbent ballast and railings along the track.

A good portion of the noise generated by ground-level transportation can be screened out by using baffles, such as stands of trees, or embankments, which channel the sound up instead of out. Embankment effects can be achieved by building up the land around the right-of-way, depressing the right-of-way below the ground level, or by placing it entirely underground. The disadvantage of adding an embankment is that it increases the size of the road, and thus also increases the probability that it will stand out unattractively from its environment. Lowering the right-of-way increases the cost, and building or digging a tunnel multiples the cost several times.

For air traffic, the use of trees and other baffles can reduce the noise levels of the airports themselves, but their use and effectiveness is limited by safety factors and the fact that once an airplane leaves the ground, such methods become totally ineffective. Modifications in engine takeoff and landing procedures, however, have helped to reduce aircraft noise. Newer-model aircraft use engines especially designed to reduce noise levels. Los Angeles and other major airports have also modified flight patterns around their airports, changing takeoff and landing approaches to reduce noise. There are, nonetheless, limits to what can be done about noise pollution. Some changes have caused outcries from pilots and airlines who say that safety is being imperiled for noise abatement purposes.

Most of the transportation systems discussed in this volume involve the use of some petroleum product for fuel: gasoline is burned by cars, kerosene by jets, and diesel fuel by nonelectric rail units and buses. Electrically operated systems like BART also generally burn petroleum products or coal at a central plant, unless the source of their electricity is nuclear or hydroelectric. In the early 1970s, over half of the particles, gases, and acids released into the atmosphere over the United States came from automobiles, trucks, and buses. The automobile accounts for the lion's share of that amount. Aircraft and trains did not add significantly to the overall figures, as only relatively small numbers of units were involved, but areas close to rail lines and airports are faced with fallout of particles and the noxious smell of exhaust. Jets burn prodigious amounts of fuel on takeoff. Electrically operated vehicles burn fuel at central locations. But, generally, the greater the number of vehicles passing a given point, the greater the amount of fumes and settling particles emitted will be. Thus, general-use freeways and airports cause the greatest problem, and rail and bus-only routes the least. The more operating units a city has—including trains, trucks, cars, buses, and airplanes—the greater its overall air pollution problem will be.

Destruction of Valuable Properties

Valuable properties may be destroyed by rights-of-way passing through or too close to them. The term *valuable property* denotes any structure or area which is used or desired by the community or by some significant portion of it and which is therefore valued by the community. Valuable properties include recreational areas and landmarks. *Destruction* denotes not merely complete or partial physical devastation of a property, but also loss of value short of for-feiture. For example, the physical structure of a building or a park might be saved in whole or in part, but be ruined for its purposes by noise, pollution, or any of the other effects mentioned above. The Overton Park and San Francisco Embarcadero Freeway cases provide excellent examples of controversy over destruction of valuable properties. In both of these cases, freeway construction meant that the value of a park or landmark would be ruined.

It is usually tempting for planners to route roads or rails through parks because this tends to dislocate the least number of people and lower the costs of land acquisition, since parks are already public lands. But cost factors may be deceptive in the long run. Particularly in the case of freeway construction, the space needed for rights-of-way can effectively obliterate a park, or at least reduce the availability of park lands to people in the area, and the city moves a step closer to being a concrete desert. When freeway plans require removal of a park in the older portions of many cities, cities often try to purchase re-placement park land. But land is often unavailable near areas served by the old park. Besides, trees take time to grow, and it may take decades to replace fully an established park.

In situations where there appears to be no alternative to passing through or near a park or other property, adverse effects can be lessened by depressing the level of the right-of-way or by digging or otherwise creating a tunnel under-neath the property. These methods naturally entail additional expense and assume that the endangered property is large enough or valuable enough to be worth saving.

Costs of freeways rise quickly when excavation is required, particularly when rights-of-way are placed fully underground. In the Overton Park case, the cost of a depressed roadway would be $26 million, while building the cut and cover tunnel proposed by the Department of Transportation would cost $160 million, including the costs of relandscaping. Digging a conventional tunnel would increase the costs still more.

Rail and bus mass transit systems tend to take up much less space than freeways and, as a result, to cause less disruption. In large part, this is true because more routes are available to mass transit systems, which have reduced right-of-way requirements. Also, where the right-of-way must pass a valuable property, tunneling or lowering the road or rail level is considerably less expensive than lowering an expressway would be. In the case of the BART system, citizens of Berkeley were able to abosrb on their own the incremental costs of placing their portion of the transit system underground and out of sight. In Memphis, on the other hand, the state of Tennessee balked at footing 10 percent of the bill for putting a highway below grade because the cost of doing so would amount to over six times the expense of grade-level construction.

General Land-Use Effects

Probably the greatest and most complex problems having to do with transportation systems are their land-use effects. These range from short-term effects such as the transformation of the large areas required for roadbeds and allied structures, to long-term effects involving the various ways the systems will alter the development of a city. Each transportation mode effects cities in different ways, repatterning land use and changing the direction and density of a city's growth.

Airports and highways require the greatest tracts of land for their facilities and so produce the greatest short-range land-use changes. Highways built to handle the increased numbers of vehicles tend to induce space loss in the core of cities. More parking lots and driving space on streets are needed. In addition, freeway interchanges can cover up to eighty acres and more of land, which is then unusable for other purposes.

Airports, particularly, require large sections of land. An airport designed for use by today's jumbo jets takes up land by the square mile for its runways and plant, not to mention the supporting structures not immediately adjacent to the airport. These include extensive complementary transportation systems, usually including freeways, to transport passengers between the airport and the cities it serves. Furthermore, height restrictions for structures must be enforced for miles in front of each runway to lessen the chances of aircraft collisions against buildings.

Bus or rail systems have considerably less short-term impact. Bus systems often use existing roads and require little else in the way of territory, unless they are operating in areas where the population is highly dispersed, in which case central collection points with parking facilities are sometimes used to increase efficiency. Rail systems also take up significantly less space than freeways, and, like buses, their supporting structures are limited to boarding stations and parking lots.

In the longer term, however, bus and rail mass transit, freeways, and airports all influence the way in which a city develops.

Cities which develop around major freeway systems tend to be more spread out and less dense than others. This is because the automobile requires space for parking, both in the central city and the suburbs. Also, the auto allows people to live farther away from shopping areas, work, and so on, because the car can take them where they need to go at any time, without great inconvenience. What results is urban sprawl. Houston and Los Angeles are typical examples.

The parking space problem also results in the diffusion or elimination of a city's central business district (CBD). When a freeway passes through rather than around a CBD, it forces the banks, department stores, restaurants, and other businesses within the CBD to accommodate parked cars and thus to spread away from each other to admit the requisite parking facilities.

There is some reason to believe that freeway growth perpetuates itself—and urban sprawl—by preventing the establishment of new CBDs and breaking up existing ones. Expansion of the freeway system instead of the addition of mass transit becomes necessary when there is public demand for better and faster commuter conduits to dispersed destinations or when housing patterns change so that increasing numbers of people are housed across town from their places of work. When such conditions occur, freeways become overloaded. Mass transit is generally not a wise alternative because neither residential areas nor destinations are concentrated enough (due to the freeway) to make a transit system efficient. A number of strategies, like devising central collection points, have been tried in order to improve the effectiveness of bus systems, but they have met with only limited success.

The only cities in the United States where rail mass transit has worked well have been those where freeway systems could not possibly serve the CBD adequately, like New York and Chicago, or where freeways have been rejected as an alternative, like San Francisco. Chicago and New York each employ so many people in their largely vertical CBDs that the number of freeway lanes necessary to move them all there by car would take up most of the space, for miles on end, around the CBDs.

Characteristically, the development pattern for mass transit, especially rail mass transit, is along densely populated corridors radiating outward from the central city. This is of course truer of rail than of bus mass transit, because buses are less restricted to their customary routes. If established in time, mass transit systems can reduce urban sprawl, take up less space, and preserve the concentration of the central business district.

How airports affect city development is less clear-cut. But a few general points can be made about them. First, new airports tend to be large ones which generally require freeways to handle ground traffic to and from terminals. Second, these freeways speed up access to open areas between airports and the cities they serve. Third, if these areas are zoned for development, industry will develop there, and people will follow, simply because the roads increase accessibility. Thus, construction of an airport near a city will eventually cause the city to grow out to meet it, and the peril of congestion is reintroduced. This has occurred at the Los Angeles airport and is now occurring around the Dallas-Fort Worth Regional Airport, where the area near the airport has become an industrial district which is attracting people in ever greater numbers.

Other Effects

Other effects include changes in climatic conditions, water tables, and runoff patterns. These are all long-range effects which may take many years to manifest themselves. Some of the climatic effects of the mass use of the automobile are only now beginning to be suspected, even though mass use of the auto began to develop fifty years ago.

Climatic effects include changes in rainfall and temperature. There has been concern among researchers over the past few years that the great cloud of pollutants in the atmosphere, much of it exhaust from transportation vehicles, may be causing a "greenhouse" effect, which in turn is increasing the overall temperature of the earth. The danger of such an effect, if it exists, is that a change of just a few degrees over time could cause massive melting of the polar ice caps, bringing on flooding of low-lying coastal regions like most of Florida.

Another effect is an increase in rainfall downwind from cities which emit high levels of pollutants into the atmosphere. Apparently, particles entering the atmosphere seed the clouds and cause more rainfall than otherwise would be normal. Again, much of the pollution comes from transport exhaust. In some regions—like the area south of Chicago—increased rainfall has produced problematic flooding.

Those vast tracts of land covered with concrete, our transportation systems, have also had major effects on water runoff and water tables. The water that runs off freeways, runways, and so on, does not have an opportunity to soak into the ground. This has two effects. First of all, it can increase the incidence of flooding by overfilling the natural streams in an area. Creeks and streams in the region around Austin, Texas, for example, have been overflowing their banks more often in the last ten years than ever before. The floods appear to be caused in part by the growth of the paved city and the concomitant reduction of ground areas for natural seepage.

The second effect is that quick runoff can slow the replenishment of the water table. Houston, Texas, has been slowly sinking over the last few years as the city has drawn water out of the water table faster than the reduced seepage can replace it.

Conclusion

All transportation systems take up space for structures, make noise while operating, and burn fuel. Most of them are highly visible. These characteristics and their by-products of visual blight and smog, coupled with the necessity for operating these systems in densely populated areas, create effects which citizens deem undesirable and so set the stage for conflict between transportation planners and public-spirited populations.

In general, where preserving or restoring environmental quality is rated a high priority, mass transit systems seem preferable to freeways. Mass transit systems operate fewer locomotive units than freeways, require less space, and are therefore less damaging to established communities and properties. Potentially, they produce less smog. They tend to reduce urban sprawl and encourage the development of central business districts. Changes in water tables, runoff patterns, and climatic conditions are also lessened.

But progress is being made in alleviating many of the environmental problems caused by every sort of transportation system: new, quieter engines reduce noise from airports; advances in materials technology allow bridges and viaducts to assume more graceful forms: and so forth. Nevertheless, the sheer size of most of these systems, and the need for them to operate within densely populated cities, requires that planners and citizens be fully aware of the environmental costs and benefits of all possible alternatives.

Bibliography

Anthrop, Donald F. *Noise Pollution*. Lexington, Mass.: D.C. Heath and Company, 1973.

Boyce, David E.; Day, Norman D.; and McDonald, Chris. *Metropolitan Plan Making*. Philadelphia: Regional Science Research Institute, 1970.

Buel, Ronald A. *Dean End: The Automobile in Mass Transportation*. Englewood Cliffs, N.J.: Prentice-Hall, Inc., 1972.

Burby, John. *The Great American Motion Sickness*. Boston: Little, Brown, 1971.

Dick, Merwin H. "A Change in the Weather Batters, and Baffles, the Railroads." *Railway Age*, 13 August 1973.

Levin, Melvin R., and Abend, Norman A. *Bureaucrats in Collision: Case Studies in Area Transportation Planning.* Cambridge: The MIT Press, 1971.

Manheim, Marvin L., et. al. *The Impacts of Highways Upon Environmental Values.* Cambridge: MIT Urban Systems Laboratory, 1969.

Paquette, Radnor J.; Ashford, Norman; and Wright, Paul H. *Transportation Engineering.* New York: The Ronald Press Company, 1972.

Rapuano, Michael, et al. *The Freeway in the City.* Washington: U.S. Government Printing Office, 1968.

Reische, Diana, ed. *Problems of Mass Transportation.* New York: The H.W. Wilson Company, 1970.

Robinson, John. *Highways and Our Environment.* New York: McGraw-Hill, 1971.

Salmon, V., and Oleson, S.K. *Noise Control in the Bay Area Rapid Transit System.* Menlo Park, Cal.: Stanford Research Institute, 1966.

Shurcliff, William A. *S/S/T and Sonic Boom Handbook.* New York: Ballantine Books, 1970.

8 Social Aspects

Lamartine Street, in the city of Boston, runs through the working-class district of the Jamaica Plain neighborhood. A scattering of blacks and Puerto Ricans live there, but mostly the population is white and Catholic, like the rest of the city's population. If you ask residents where they live, they will tell you the parish's name before the name of the street. Not too long ago the character of Lamartine changed radically—from a colorful street lined with two- and three-story commercial and residential brick structures to one whose odd-numbered houses look out over a flat wasteland. To highway planners, Lamartine Street was simply a right-of-way for Interstate 95.

Some houses on the even-numbered side of the street remain, but most have been razed. Number 270, for example, is a yellow house with brown trim and a neat garden. Its occupants are an elderly couple. Their home was not needed for the highway, but they saw and heard the bulldozers rip up their neighbors' homes all the way to Number 216. Number 216 and the house behind it are gutted. Strewn all over the adjoining yard is the abandoned evidence of a family's personal life, from the kind of beans they ate to the sort of television they owned. There is a Maytag washer, a green scatter rug, a pair of size-nine black French Shriner shoes, and old copies of *Field and Stream* and *Sports Illustrated*. Behind the house, lying in a large field that was once a neighborhood, are a mangled tricycle, the center of a broken record featuring Blue Barron and His Orchestra in "Cruising Down the River," and two-thirds of another record, a collection of Chirstmas carols by Bing Crosby. The relics represent a culture known as White Ethnic Urban American, a bit of civilization plowed under in the interest of progress and Interstate 95.

In the planning of today's transportation systems, usually too much emphasis is placed on technical and economic considerations and too little thought is given to the people directly affected by the systems. Displacement and relocation of residents and the civic and commercial disruption of neighborhoods are real side effects of mass transit construction. The indigent and the black are often affected by the type of transport system that is built, and most often it is their neighborhoods that are sacrificed soonest.

Displacement and Relocation

The Federal Housing Authority stipulates that when families are displaced from their homes because of government action they should be relocated by the appropriate local public agency in affordable dwellings that meet statutory requirements of cleanliness, safety, and decency. The principal consideration in the FHA's concept of relocation is to provide compensation for the net value of real estate appropriated. Recently, a report published by the Advisory Commission on Intergovernmental Relations has questioned the adequacy of the FHA's rule and suggested that there are additional cost burdens which are direct consequences of transport projects and should be compensated for, just as the costs of the appropriated real estate are.

An example of the sort of assistance currently available can be found in the relocation programs of Texas. In accordance with the Federal Highway Act of 1968, the state highway department must provide displaced persons with lists of relocation dwellings, information regarding security deposits, down payments, and interest rates, maps of relocation areas showing where schools, parks, shopping areas and public transportation routes are located, time and price schedules for public transportation services, and whatever other relocation information might be useful. The state highway department must make compensatory payments to cover the moving costs incurred by eligible individuals, families, businesses, farm operations, and nonprofit organizations displaced from property acquired by the state for highway construction. Individuals and families must move to dwellings no further than fifty miles away and must submit two bids by responsible moving companies to the highway department prior to the move, or elect to receive $100 plus an amount computed on the basis of the number of rooms formerly occupied. Homeowners who lived in their property are entitled to supplemental payments up to $5,000 to acquire a replacement dwelling which meets the department's standards of safety, cleanliness, and decency. Renters may receive rent supplements of up to $1,500 in twenty-four months. The department also assumes the incidental expenses involved in transferring real property to state and local agencies for construction.

Relocation procedures like these are developed by middle-class professionals and thus assume the self-sufficiency of the family-household. In many urban areas, however, large numbers of physically individual households function symbiotically with other households connected by strong bonds of kinship or peer-group membership. If single households are relocated so that the other households with whom they interact are inaccessible, negative social and emotional consequences may result. People can come together again by car or public transportation, but only if they are relocated with sensitivity to the sociological realities involved.

Often, relocation officials and low-income urban residents differ in their views of the physical and social "standardness" of housing. Dwellings which authorities define as physically standard may be located in areas that residents consider socially undesirable. Because social criteria are usually more important to people with low incomes then physical criteria, they may reject the units offered to them by relocation officials. On the other hand, they may relocate themselves in dwelling units that are substandard by federal provisions, but not by the priority of their own social values.

As a rule, the scheduling of relocations is dictated by the requirements of the clearance program. If relocation takes longer than expected, it may force officials to interpret the federal relocation provisions in the narrowest manner and limit the number of apartment choices given to each family to what is strictly required by law. Given the differences in housing standards held by officials and residents, some people may be forced to move into dwelling units and neighborhoods they do not want to live in. Others may be hurried into panicky voluntary relocation, which may have the same results.

Because of the shortage of rental housing, some people are encouraged to buy houses in the suburbs at prices beyond their ability to pay. Former homeowners find that new mortgages can only be had at close to double the interest rates on their old homes. Others find that they have reached the age at which no bank will lend to them. The relocation services and compensatory payments required of the Department of Public Works are only token compensation for hardships inflicted.

Landlords who were able to live modestly from the rentals of one or more buildings lose their incomes. The amount of money they receive for these buildings is usually not enough to permit them to purchase others.

By destroying places of employment, highways displace workers. Jobs are lost. A good number of these jobs are lost altogether since many, if not most, of the businesses commonly relocate outside the area. Many of the more marginal firms—like small stores that have built up a clientele over the years—go out of business completely. Their owners may be too old to be hired by other employers or to acquire loans to start new businesses.

Relocation also discriminates racially. In 1970, 18 percent of those dislocated were nonwhite, while only 12.5 percent of the population was nonwhite. Studies show that blacks pay more for their relocation and, even when they have incomes enabling them to afford standard private housing, often face obstacles in discriminatory real-estate financing and zoning practices, which reduce the supply of lands available to build on and of houses to purchase or rent. Most nonwhites above the income level necessary to qualify for low-rent public housing find it more difficult to borrow than do white families of similar economic means. Forced into already crowded, substandard housing facilities, the displaced nonwhite families create new and aggravate old ghettos.

Since relocation procedures do not allow for the transfer of whole social systems, the ensuing shock from the relocation process is itself likely to increase the negative effect of moving, especially for those people who have never lived anywhere else, and whose social and emotional ties have been established entirely within their old neighborhood.

A survey of residents' attitudes toward the proposed Inner Loop in

Washington, D.C., concluded that involuntary moves are upsetting, that individuals with sentimental attachments to specific neighborhood features often crowd into adjacent, similar neighborhoods with losses to all, and that major physical neighborhood changes require major social and psychological adjustments.

In a similar survey relating to Boston's West End project, the findings were that forced relocation is a highly disruptive and disturbing experience, a crisis potentially endangering the mental health of many people. Often, all the symptoms of grief syndrome are present, and grief reaction is strongest among the working class, particularly those strongly committed to their neighborhoods. Reactions are expressed in terms of painful loss, continued longing and depression, a sense of helplessness, and psychological or social distress. A companion study concluded that the effects of the uprooting experience, the loss of familiar places and persons, and the difficulties of adjusting to and accepting new living environments may be far more serious relocation issues than changes in housing status.

The Overton Park controversy in Memphis, Tennessee, involved more than objections to building a freeway through a park. One of the proposed routes was ruled out as an alternative by Secretary of Transportation William T. Coleman, Jr., because it would displace 147 families.

Displacement creates special problems for large families. It is difficult for them to relocate because there is always a shortage of large units in low-rent public housing. Large units are in short supply in the private housing market as well, particularly where housing codes are enforced with respect to increases in occupancy.

In addition to suffering all the ordinary trials of relocation, the elderly have special housing problems stemming from conditions associated with the process of aging. It is difficult for them to adjust to the increased demands that a move makes of them—both physically, when their strengths are diminishing, and psychologically, when the pattern of their lives has been a slow withdrawal from social activity. Because generally they must live on fixed low incomes and because the supply of housing attuned to their needs is so small, the elderly are especially vulnerable to disruption. For the nonwhite elderly, the problems are compounded. All in all, the elderly represent the group most difficult to relocate satisfactorily. The problem is serious because, in many cities, production of housing suitable for older persons and within their economic means is not keeping pace with the rate at which their dwellings are being torn down to accommodate changes in urban land uses.

All elderly people face an uncertain future. The specters of serious and perhaps final illness, increased living costs, and the loss of close friends and relatives trouble many of them. The elderly live on their memories of the past. When friendships, familiar blocks, and accustomed shopkeepers must be abandoned because relocation is a necessity, the prospect of having to recreate those essential social fibers brings the terror of the future into sharp and relentless focus, heightening their sense of aloneness.

Individualized adjustments to the physical limitations of advanced years may be destroyed by relocation. Mrs. B has a neighbor who does supermarket shopping for her once a week. The janitor in Mr. L's building has known him for years and does all sorts of repair work for him cheerfully and gratis. Mrs. M's niece lives in the same building and checks on her needs every day or so.

Many relocation officials may be aware of the complex problems which face the elderly. Assistance in meeting them, however, is rarely offered unless a clear-cut issue is involved.

No one anticipates with pleasure the distressing experience of moving. The process involves apartment hunting, packing, movers, and a chaotic arrival at a new residence. Anxiety over relocations may develop even before the actual need to relocate is established. A newspaper story or preliminary door-to-door surveys by officials can engulf a neighborhood very quickly in alarming rumors of impending demolition. Elderly people, who have little to do and who are relatively isolated from responsible community leaders, are more susceptible to the fears caused by rumors than others more in touch with community affairs. The time lag between public awareness of demolition plans and the presence in the neighborhood of an official agency which can answer questions and correct misinformation creates ample opportunity for widespread panic.

When the time to relocate finally arrives, the elderly person is faced with exhausting and, in some respects, unreasonable demands. He must make tiring trips to other parts of the city in order to inspect apartments. Too often, the relocator may have made little attempt to consider the special needs of a person advanced in years. The elderly person, or couple, who must look at an apartment without guidance after an exhausting trip to a strange neighborhood is in a poor position to make a rational decision about it.

Once an apartment is accepted, other hazards may develop. Furniture may have to be sold or purchased quickly. Costly mistakes are made by persons who are inexperienced and time-pressured. Movers have to be found, again very likely without guidance.

In a great many instances, an elderly person lives alone. Moving day creates conflicting demands. Someone must be on hand to supervise the movers when they pack the truck; someone must be on hand to receive them. What might prove annoying to the energetic younger person can be overwhelming for the elderly. Once the relocated person takes up residence in his new home, his contact with the relocating agency, however minimal, ceases. There is no one to assist him in finding new service establishments, stores, churches, doctors, and dental clinics.

Relocation efforts daily discover people who have major physical or psychological handicaps. These men and women may lack the basic resources to reestablish themselves. Their special needs were either overlooked by the community through ignorance or indifference or taken care of in idiosyncratic ways. Nevertheless, the problems of these people are too often avoided by the relocation official, who sends them to new residences to make out as best they can.

Some handicapped elderly people manage at least a marginal existence by finding important supports in their neighborhood. Miss D, a rooming-house tenant, suffered advancing arthritis. It had become almost impossible for her to leave her room. In addition, her psychological difficulties led her to live the life of a recluse. A trusted maid, employed by the rooming house, and a sympathetic landlord made it possible for her to survive with a modicum of dignity. The maid shopped and cooked for her twice a week. With the connivance of the landlord, ruses were employed to get Miss D out of her room from time to time so it could be cleaned. Unless the relocation agency could somehow arrange to duplicate this kind of assistance, Miss D would have to be institutionalized.

A special study conducted jointly by the University of Pennsylvania's Institute for Urban Studies and the National Association of Housing and Redevelopment Officials analyzed the problems faced by elderly persons who had been relocated. An interim report described the many sorts of charges that relocated residents had made against relocation agencies. They involved last-minute notifications, failure to distribute information about rights and procedures, requirements that displaced families seek assistance on their own or come to the agency for it, and so forth. The major complaint, however, was that householders had to reconstruct their lives quickly and under duress. The worst aspect of relocation for many of the elderly was that they had been obliged to break those habits and forfeit those friendships which had long sustained the pattern of their lives.

Disruption

Highways do not simply remove housing from the market. If badly located they destroy something far more difficult to replace—established neighborhoods that enjoy a deep sense of community. The casual motorist driving down the proposed Inner Belt route in Cambridge, Massachusetts, might not see anything he would identify in a physical sense as a community, but the residents of Brookline and Elm streets have a history of shared experiences and mutual assistance.

A community develops in an area when certain behavioral and perceptual relationships exist among the residents. These are exhibited in patterns of conduct and interaction—such as visiting, shared use of local facilities, and active participation in local organizations. The perceptual relationships are those feelings or attitudes that influence that behavior. They involve psychological identification with the neighborhood and a positive evaluation of it.

Community cohesion, or the attraction between families and individuals in a nieghborhood, may be disrupted in several different ways—by increased noise, dirt, or congestion during highway construction and operations, by removal of vital neighborhood services or of residents needed to assure adequate neighborhood facilities, or by confining citizen movement to activities within the community.

When the BART system in San Francisco was planned, citizens of Berkeley wisely opposed a proposed elevated trackway through the business district on the grounds that it would create a sociological barrier between the east and west sides of the city. The major fear was that the tracks would split Berkeley along racial lines. The citizens were set so strongly against the original plan that 80 percent of the voters approved a proposal for making the Berkeley section of BART a subway and increasing their own taxes to pay for it.

Highways may also affect community cohesion in a positive way. For example, community cohesion may be strengthened if a highway forms a border protecting the community from encroachment by an undesirable land use. Highway proximity may also ease access to community services or provide valuable visual exposure for community service centers.

More often, however, even when a highway does not plow through the middle of a community, the damage is considerable. Boston's Central Artery is an example of what highway critics call a "Chinese Wall"—a physical and psychological barrier isolating a nieghborhood from its shopping areas, churches, schools, and friends.

The Brookline-Elm streets area of Cambridge (the proposed Inner Belt route) is unusually well integrated, ethnically and racially. Racial and ethnic harmony appear to be a reality there, rather than a cliché. Many of the residents walk to work and their children walk to school. But only about half of the homeowners have improved their properties in the past decade; the rest have refrained from doing so in fear of losing their investments to highway clearance.

Transportation and Poverty

Current changes in urban structures and urban transportation systems have provided significant improvements in the mobility of a majority of urban dwellers. At the same time, these very changes have lessened the access to opportunities and impaired the mobility of a significant fraction of the poor.

Before the mid-1940s, a city's activities were concentrated in its central business district. Concentration made it possible for low-income workers to have access to most of the job locations—clustered with housing and transit service—in the central city. Today, improved technology and a rising, expanding economic base have helped to create rapid growth in the size and geographical expansiveness of cities.

When metropolitan industries began decentralizing, low-skilled employment areas began to be located on the outskirts of urban areas. The ever more frequent substitution of trucks for railroad freight cars and the burgeoning use of airlines in lieu of railroads for passenger travel shifted the greater part of employment opportunities in intercity transportation away from the central city. The development of trucking, piggybacking, and other new techniques for moving freight from city to city made factory location near a railroad marshaling yard no longer necessary for low-cost, high-quality freight service. In addition, many industries left the cities because they needed large tracts of unencumbered land to set up efficient one-story manufacturing plants.

By taking the bulk of blue-collar commuter traffic away from the central business district, this rapid growth of the cities has improved the mobility of the majority but it has lessened the mobility of low-income groups, whose job locations were moved out of walking distance and away from transit service.

When the majority of urban dwellers became less dependent on public transit, transit patronage and, thus, transit service began a steady decline. In fact, public transit systems have been declining ever since World War II. Today, transit patronage is about two-thirds of what it was in 1940. And this has occurred despite considerable growth in urban population over the past decade. The explanation lies in the fact that an increasing proportion of the urban population is choosing to make trips by way of automobile. To a considerable extent, this is the result of steady increases in auto ownership. In 1950, six out of every ten U.S. households possessed one or more private automobiles. By 1967, the ratio was nearly eight over ten. These figures indicate what is certainly a trend. Today the majority of urban employees have turned to modes of private transportation, leaving the inadequate public mass transit systems to serve a not so silent minority.

Still, poor city dwellers continue to depend very greatly on public transit. The automobile, nearly indispensable in much of urban America, is a very expensive mode of transportation. In most circumstances, the high initial capital outlay and the operating costs of a private automobile are a heavy strain on the budgets of hard-pressed, low-income households. Moreover, the acquisition of an efficient private automobile (one without high maintenance costs) requires considerable financing, a chronic problem for the poor. The average operating cost of an automobile, including sunk costs and out-of-pocket expenses, was 11.77 cents per mile in 1966. In 1975 it was estimated at 15 cents per mile. Statistics on car ownership among the poor may paint a more favorable picture than the facts generally prove. Poor people most often own bad cars. Many are inadequate for long-distance commuting or expressway operation or, worse yet, are uninsured.

Currently, metropolitan public transit is severely inadequate in meeting the needs of the urban poor. As a general rule, modern-day bus transit follows the routes of the old streetcar lines. As this pattern suggests, it is the area most immediate to the central business district which is covered best. If an individual on the outskirts of the transit service wishes to travel to a destination also on the outskirts, he is required to take a radial bus into the central business district and then transfer to another bus going back out to his destination. Direct routes are not provided because the majority tend to use automobiles for lateral trips in the suburbs. Current transit lines do not coincide with the lines the low-skilled workers desire.

The popular concept that providing subsidies for public urban transit will help the poor proves less than self-evident. Most of the new systems, like the BART system in San Francisco and transit extensions in Boston, provide the poor with only nominal benefits. Both the San Francisco and Boston systems are heavily subsidized from property tax monies, which is heavily regressive. Virtually all the benefits accrue to high-income suburbs and central employment centers. These new transit systems do practically nothing to improve accessibility between centrally located ghettoes and suburban employment centers.

Transportation and Race

While changes in the spatial structure of metropolitan areas and in transit systems have created problems for all poverty households, their impact on low-income blacks has been especially serious. Housing market segregation deprives the low-income black of many of the adjustments available to low-income whites. If the job of a low-income white worker shifts to the suburbs, he is usually able to follow it. In many cases, he will be able to relocate his residence to be near a transit line serving his workplace. This is not to say that he will have an easy time finding suitable housing, but the evidence available suggests that most low-income whites employed in suburban areas are able to make some kind of reasonable adjustment.

The low-income black is seldom so fortunate. He will find it difficult to move out of the ghetto, regardless of his income or family situation. If his job moves to the suburbs, he may not be able to follow it. So, for him the cost, coverage, and service characteristics of the transportation system are especially critical. Even if his suburban workplace is served by a transit line, he often is unable to move to a neighborhood served by that particular transit line. Usually, the transit company serving the suburban workplace will not be the same one serving the ghetto. If the ghetto dweller is able to reach a suburban workplace at all by public transit, the trip will usually be expensive, involve a long and indirect route, and require numerous time-consuming transfers. A job must be uncommonly desirable for the low-income black to make the trip by transit or to pay the additional costs of automobile transportation. In some cases, his income will be no lower if he refuses the job and remains unemployed. If he is extraordinarily lucky, he may be able to form a car pool with fellow workers and share the expense of the long-distance trip from his neighborhood, but the probability of such an arrangement is reduced by limitations on his choice of residence and the remoteness of most suburban workplaces from his home in the city.

John F. Kain's study on housing segregation and black employment suggests that housing market segregation may have cost Chicago blacks as many as 25,000 jobs and Detroit blacks as many as 9,000 jobs. The Kain study estimates are based on 1952 and 1956 data. Given the accelerating decentralization of employment, it seems possible that job losses are even greater today.

In reporting on the causes of the 1965 Watts riots, the McCone Commission concluded that the most serious immediate problem facing the black citizen in Los Angeles was employment—securing and holding a job that provides an opportunity for earning a decent livelihood, a chance to earn the means of supporting himself and his family, dignity, and the chance to regard himself as a member of the community in a true sense.

The McCone Commission suggested that while serious lack of skill and overt discrimination were major causes of high black unemployment (two to three times the average rate), the geographic isolation of South Central Los Angeles and the inadequate and costly public transportation existing throughout the metropolitan area seriously restricted residents of black neighborhoods like Watts. At the time of the study, no direct connections existed with other areas of the city where major sources of employment were located. Four separate bus lines were operating within the area, requiring several bus changes and the payment of several fares in order to leave it. Clearly, the lack of adequate transportation severely handicapped the residents of Watts in seeking and holding jobs, attending schools, shopping, and fulfilling other needs.

As with so many other problems confronting our society today, it appears that "transportation and poverty" is a euphemism for "transportation and race." This is not to say that the white poor are not hindered by inadequate mobility, but rather that the problems of blacks, in particular, are acute and likely to worsen in the absence of positive public action.

Up to now, whether planners have taken it upon themselves to build a road, relocate a neighborhood, or map a transit system, social considerations have taken a back seat to solving the technical and economic problems of transportation projects. But as case after case has shown, the social aspects of change have been the root causes of controversy and conflict and, as such, deserve the respectful attention of everyone concerned with the improvement of mass transport systems.

Bibliography

Automobile Manufacturers Association. *Automobile Facts and Figures, 1968.*
     Detroit: Automobile Manufacturers Association, Inc., 1968.
Bollens, John C., and Schmandt, Henry J. *The Metropolis; Its People, Politics,*
     and Economic Life. New York: Harper and Row, 1965.
Chinitz, Benjamin. *City and Suburb: The Economics of Metropolitan Growth.*

Englewood Cliffs, N.J.: Prentice-Hall, Inc., 1964.

Essays on the Problems Faced in the Relocation of Elderly Persons. University of Pennsylvania: Institute for Urban Studies.

Gans, Herbert J. "The Human Implications of Current Redevelopment and Relocation Planning." *Journal of the American Institute of Planners* 25 (1959): 15-25.

Governor's Commission on the Los Angeles Riots. *Violence in the City—An End or a Beginning.* Los Angeles Cal. 1965.

Highway Research Board. "Community Values and Socioeconomic-Impact." Highway Research Record 277, 1969.

Kain, John F. "Housing Segregation, Negro Employment, and Metropolitan Decentralization." *The Quarterly Journal of Economics* 82 (May 1968).

Kain, John F., and Meyer, John R. *Interrelationships of Transportation and Poverty.* Cambridge: Harvard University Press, 1958.

Lupo, Alan; Colcord, Frank; and Fowler, Edmund P., *Rites-of-Way.* Boston: Little, Brown, 1971.

Meyer, John R.; Kain, John F.; and Wohl, Martin. *The Urban Transportation Problem.* Cambridge: Harvard University Press, 1965.

Niebank, Paul L., and Pope, John B. *The Elderly in Older Urban Areas.* University of Pennsylvania: Institute for Environmental Studies, 1965.

Owen, Wilfred. *The Metropolitan Transportation Problem.* Washington, D.C.: Brookings Institution, 1966.

"Surveying Highway Impact." *Environment* 14 (November 1972).

U.S. Department of Housing and Urban Development. *Interim Report, HUD Project No. Mass-MTD-3.* Cambridge: Harvard University Press, 1968.

U.S. Department of Transportation. *Social and Economic Effects of Highways.* Washington, D.C., Federal Highway Commission, 1974.

Transportation, Politics, and Government

Transportation and politics have been inseparable throughout American history. Ships opened the American continent for settlement, and ships were the political instruments used by the European monarchs to control trade and extract profits from the colonies. The English Acts of Trade and Navigation were one of the primary elements in fomenting the colonial rebellion. Even after the republic was established, transportation issues continued to be political ones. After the Revolutionary War, the fulfillment of the United States' manifest destiny was linked closely to cooperation between state and territorial governments and the privately owned railway and canal companies.

From the very start, it was the states, or territories, which, in cooperation with private entrepreneurs, played the major role in developing transportation systems. Although vitally interested in the extension of the transportation web across the United States, the federal government followed a line of Jacksonian democracy, that federal intervention in internal improvements was a violation of states' rights. Nevertheless, the federal government gave substantial subsidies in the form of route surveys, duty remission, right-of-way grants, and land grants to private corporations so that transportation systems could be built.

During the initial phases of development for the various transportation modes, the entrepreneur and public interests were often compatible. Seeking profit, businessmen and new settlers willingly cooperated in the development of transportation systems. Once the systems were completed, interests split. The entrepreneurs wished to maximize their return on investments while the public wished to minimize the cost of transportation services. When either or both sides resorted to the political process to achieve their goals, a means of forced resolution was necessary. One way to resolve conflicts was through the creation of regulatory agencies.

The Interstate Commerce Commission (ICC), for instance, was established to resolve conflicts between the railroads and their clients. In the 1870s, the railroads were expanding and were attempting to maximize their return on investments. The economy of the midwestern United States was agricultural. Farmers depended on the railroads to transport their products to the urban markets. They, too, wished to maximize their profits and so wanted to pay the lowest possible rates for rail transport. The conflict between the railroads and the farmers flared when agricultural prices declined. The farmers sought relief by pressing for legislation to control railroad rates. Several states enacted laws which subjected the railroads to regulation. Inasmuch as the actions of the states had no precedent, the railroads appealed to the judicial system for relief, expecting that the state laws would be invalidated. Instead of invalidating the laws, the Supreme Court recognized the federal government's responsibility to legislate and regulate transportation in order to further the commerce of the nation. The Supreme Court ruled that because the federal government had failed to fulfill its responsibility, the states could enforce the rules and regulations they deemed necessary to the welfare of the people within their jurisdictions, even though, by so doing, those outside the states would be indirectly affected. In the series of suits known as the Granger Cases, the Supreme Court refined its interpretation of the Commerce Clause of the Constitution. One outcome of the Court's rulings was that in 1887 Congress passed the Act to Regulate Commerce, which created the ICC. That act of Congress marked the beginning of the federal government's active involvement in transportation regulation.

As the federal government became more involved in the promotion and regulation of trade and transportation, it created additional agencies and bureaus to deal with these functions. Finally, in 1966, the Department of Transportation was created in an attempt to draw together under one head all the federal agencies primarily concerned with the administration and promotion of transportation.

The growth of the transportation bureaucracy has not been as dramatic at the state level as it has at the federal level. The primary growth has been in highway-related transportation operations, including the planning and construction of state road networks. The growth of city transportation agencies has only really taken place within the last quarter of this century, coinciding with the rapid urbanization prompted by the abnormal population displacements caused by World War II. More recently, petroleum fuel price rises have promoted the growth of city and county transportation agencies.

The federal government's power to regulate the transportation industries rests on sound theoretical and legal principles. Transportation enterprises perform a public service, so it follows that the various governmental bodies are responsible to some degree for regulation or administration of transportation services. As the Supreme Court noted, the legal basis for government participation is found in the Constitution's Commerce Clause. Additional justification can be found in the nature of the transportation enterprises themselves. That is, private corporations have succeeded in providing public transportation only because the public has granted them the use of public authority—specifically, the power of eminent domain—which gives these privately owned corporations public powers. The fundamental justification for government participation and regulation is found not in the rulings of the courts of the land but in legislation like that enacting the Interstate Commerce Commission, legislation designed to resolve conflicts like those which arose between the transportation entrepreneurs and the American public 100 years ago.

As American history has shown, when government assumes a responsibility, the tendency is to create a bureaucracy to discharge that responsibility. The way transportation agencies are related to the government structure (see Figure 9-1) confirms this. There is a transportation agency in each municipality, township, and county, and several at the state and federal levels as well. For the most part, all of these agencies were created to regulate. And they constitute an integral part of what the public considers the nation's transportation bureaucracy.

But how does the bureaucracy relate to public desire? Initially, transportation authorities and a majority of the public have goals which are obtainable only through the establishment of a transportation system. These goals may be to some extent mutually exclusive. That is, neither the transportation people nor the public may obtain full realization of their goals. Conflict develops. Within a democracy, revolutionary political tactics are not acceptable, so the contending sides must work within an established political framework. In the

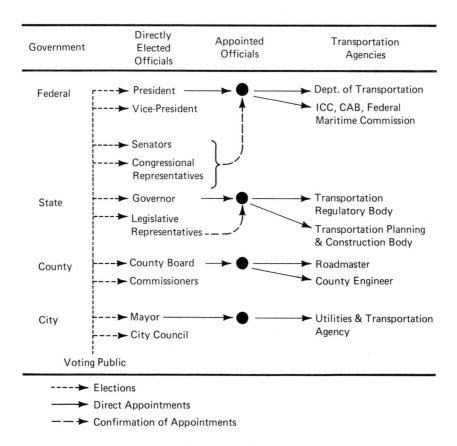

Figure 9-1. Relation of Transportation Agencies to Government Structure

United States, this framework consists of the Constitution, the electoral system, the legislative bodies, and the judicial system. To enhance its prospects for successfully achieving its goals through political means, each side will attempt to influence as many elements in the systems as it can. Although that activity may prolong the conflict and appear to unbalance the system, in reality it accounts for the dynamism of the system. The interaction of the forces will continue until, as history proves, the power of the public (from which the democratic systems derives its existence) dominates, and a solution acceptable to a majority is promulgated. At least this is how the system was meant, ideally, to work. In the real world, public interaction with decision-making elements within the bureaucracy is extremely difficult to achieve.

In Figure 9-1 we can see, graphically, the vast distance between the voting public and the persons heading the transportation agencies at every level of government. The problem is that these agencies are the bodies responsible for representing the public's interest and protecting its investments in transportation. Figure 9-1 shows the elected government officials who, allowing for slight variations, are found in every state in the union. The principal variation is found within county governments. Some areas have no county bodies, or else the functions of these bodies are administered by city-town governments. There may be a variation in the city governing entities, depending on whether the executive power is assumed by the mayor, the city council, or, in some cases, a city manager. In any case, the main point of the illustration is that only a minor segment of the government is directly elected by the American people. It is the appointed officials, and not the elected representatives, who carry on the day-to-day business of the government. Among the ranks of appointed officials are those who perform the administration and regulation of transportation.

Another important point that must be made about government agencies is that only the principal officer, or agency head, is without tenure. Today, most government employees are protected by a state or federal civil service system which provides job tenure and makes it difficult to discharge them, except for proven cause. The tenure policy in government further removes the bureaucracy from public control.

An often overlooked fact about the American government is that its structure does not have its origins entirely in the Constitution. The governorships are the oldest governmental elements, and some of the townships or county governments have been in existence for scores of years and some for over a century prior to the Declaration of Independence and the ratification of the Constitution. Certain practices associated with the older nondemocratic institutions have been carried over into our times. One example is the contribution system, which in modern times takes more nefarious forms: the private financing of political parties, the bestowing of contracts of jobs on favored parties within the private sector, and so on down the line of corrupt practices.

Except in rare cases, elected government officials are not transportation experts, nor are they aware of the complex problems associated with transportation planning. Understandably, then, the planning is being done in the agencies where the technical transportation experts are located. These individuals are removed from public supervision because they are appointed officials. Yet, it is these individuals whose jobs involve interpreting the public needs for new transportation facilities, developing the designs, and overseeing the construction.

Certainly, elected representatives are always present to protect the public interest, but elected representatives lack the technical skills and sophisticated conceptual knowledge which would enable them to understand and, thus, to criticize intelligently the experts' plans. Their ignorance reduces the likelihood of their raising objections to the projects still in the conceptual phase, and it is this phase of planning that is most problematic.

One reason why the conceptual phase of a project is indeed the most difficult has to do with the time frame for the planning phase. In the case of the MoPac expressway, the project stayed in the planning stages for over fifteen years. During that time many changes took place within the community. By the time construction was begun, it was too late to adjust or make changes in the project without incurring heavy costs. The time element in project planning is equally important in cases where delays caused by legal actions cost taxpayers millions of dollars. The high cost of delays caused by conflict is added to the price the public pays for transportation. The experts in the transportation agencies are only partly to blame. Recently, when a knowledgeable observer was asked what process a highway project in Texas must go through before the highway is built, he was unable to answer except in general terms. Although he had had years of experience observing Texas government, the inner workings of the Texas Highway Department were still a mystery to him. To many like him, the generation process for transportation projects must often appear to be almost beyond comprehension, but the process *can* be schematically represented (see Figure 9-2). The diagram shows the process by means of which a transportation project is planned, approved, and realized in most urban communities. It serves to underline the indispensable role the transportation bureaucrat has created for himself. He understands the bureaucratic process and knows how to work within the system to achieve his own desired objectives. The most important point the diagram makes is that the public's direct input into the transportation planning process is minimal. Bureaucrats work out the details of route location, financing, and construction, and elected officials are asked to rubber-stamp their approval of the project as blueprinted by transportation experts. The public voice is decidedly left out.

"But what about public hearings?" one may ask. It is normal, of course, to hold public hearings on projects prior to promulgation or implementation, but the principal witnesses who appear at them represent organized political pressure groups or lobbies for entities affected by the proposed project. These special-interest groups, whether for or against the action, seldom speak in behalf of the

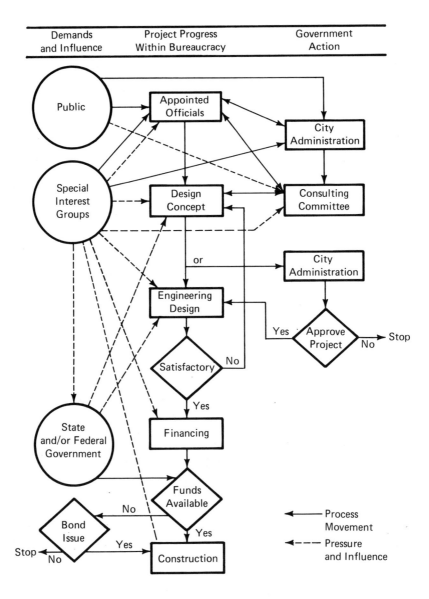

Figure 9-2. Transportation Project Generation Process

public. Ironically, the outcome of a public hearing may or may not be in the best interest of the public.

Another problem inherent to the planning process centers around the bureaucrat. Normally, bureaucrats determine what the public need is. For example, a bureaucrat responsible for maintaining and improving a state's highway network always has some project on the drawing boards. He has a vested interest in ensuring that there is sufficient work in progress to safeguard his own job. Obviously, as human beings all do, the bureaucrat has personal preferences, or priorities, for improving his city, but it is much easier for a skilled bureaucrat than for an ordinary citizen to include his own personal priorities in a planned action and get them implemented.

Bureaucratic planning normally follows the line of least resistance. For example, even though the survey for a new highway construction project indicates that it is cheaper and shorter to route the highway across Mr. Smith's $100,000 putting green than through the city park, the plan may not be drawn up that way. If Mr. Smith can mobilize sufficient political support, the new highway is more likely to run right through the middle of the park than over his green. Examples like this can be seen by anyone who is willing to ride the freeways and be objective: low-income areas and public lands have disproportionately high freeway mileage through them. Consider the routing of Interstate 35 through Austin, Texas. It is the economically and politically weak east side of Austin that has had to suffer the isolation and economic decay brought on by the highway.

As we have seen, the very political makup of transportation agencies is a major source of the public's problems in regaining some control over transportation planning. In fact, the agencies have assumed functions for which they were not chartered. They were created to regulate private enterprise, but today their main function has become to plan entire transportation systems. In the past, private entrepreneurs seeking profits planned the transportation systems they built. The entrepreneur was able to carry out his plan when it was compatible with the interests of the commercial and political centers it affected. The results of the entrepreneur's activities were economic growth, population shifts, the increased prosperity of some areas, and the reduced prosperity of others. Government transportation agencies have attempted methodically to harness these transportation phenomena in their plans so as to promote economic and population growth in some areas and relieve others of urban growth problems. The agency planners also promote new or refined rapid transportation modes to relieve urban areas of traffic congestion.

To summarize, then, the way transportation planning is being conducted by government agencies today is riddled with problems for the following reasons:

1. Elected public representatives are not transportation experts.

2. For the most part, planning is done by a bureaucracy which has a vested interest in outcomes.
3. The bureaucracy is not in tune with the real desires of the public.
4. Public hearings as they are now conducted do not provide for real public input.
5. The planning process is easily influenced by special-interest groups and politically influential individuals.
6. Because of time frames involved, the planning system is inflexible.
7. The planning system is desultory.

Earlier in this chapter, I noted that conflict between transportation authorities and the public persists until a solution acceptable to a majority of the public is found. Although the political influence of commercial interests is still strong, the entry of government into regulation has provided an acceptable partial solution to some of the problems. But the creation of a government bureaucracy which not only regulates but also assumes full responsibility for planning public transportation systems is now stimulating further conflict. Nowhere does the Constitution mention the sort of bureaucratic structure which has proliferated lately. In fact, decisions made by bureaucracies are, by their very nature, undemocratic. It is no wonder that public disapproval has shifted from the entrepreneur to the bureaucrat. The governmental entities created to protect the public interest are now the public's chief antagonists. Unless elected representatives become aware of the changes that have taken place in public reactions to the way transportation decisions are made today, many cities may find themselves with freeways that go nowhere and airports from which carriers may not fly.

Bibliography

Caldwell, Gaylon L., and Lawrence, Robert M. *American Government Today*. New York: W.W. Norton and Co., 1969.

Caro, Robert A., *The Power Broker*. New York: Knopf, 1974.

Johnson, Lyndon B. *The Choices We Face*. New York: Bantam Books, Inc., 1969.

McCleskey, Clifton. *The Government and Politics of Texas*. Boston: Little, Brown, 1963.

Mayo, Henry B. *Democratic Theory, An Introduction*. New York: Oxford University Press, 1960.

Morrison, Samuel E., and Commager, Henry S. *The Growth of the American Republic*. New York: Oxford University Press, 1962.

Pectason, J.W., and Burns, James M., eds. *Functions and Policies of American Government*. Englewood Cliffs, N.J.: Prentice-Hall, Inc., 1962.

Ribicoff, Abraham, and Newman, Jon O. *Politics: The American Way*. Boston: Allyn and Bacon, Inc., 1967.

10 Continuing Confict and Future Changes

A little over seventy years ago, Frank Norris published a book called *The Octopus*. It is a tale of California, romantically told but solidly based in the history of the central valleys where the great wheat lands of California are located. It tells of the conflict between the wheat farmers and the Southern Pacific Railroad. The farmers found themselves at the mercy of the railroad because the railroad could set the freight rate for wheat without in any way being answerable to the farmer. So the farmers rebelled. The result was the bloodshed that Frank Norris describes.

Because of the California farmers' uprising and other troubles, the federal government formed the Interstate Commerce Commission, the first federal agency for regulating transportation. Over the years, more and more federal transportation agencies were created, culminating in a full-fledged department.

Gradually, the personae of the conflict changed. Initially the farmers struggled against the power of the railroad. Or, to put it another way, the people confronted giant private enterprise. As more and more regulatory bureaucracies were created, the people began to look upon government agencies as adversaries.

Highway bureaucracies have become the most powerful public transportation agencies in the United States, primarily due to the tremendous development of highways over the last twenty years as our primary form of transportation. This development has also made highways the most controversial mode of transportation. Highways have inherent characteristics that make them the centers of debate. Highway rights-of-way, for instance, require great expanses of land to accommodate the long, straight stretches of concrete, the cloverleafs, and the access ramps. Because of the large tracts of land needed, the highway bureaucracies tend to choose what they have discovered to be the path of least resistance—the path leading through public land or historical areas. These lands are especially attractive because they are already publicly owned and generally do not require massive displacement of persons or business. The Overton Park and the Golden Gate Park Panhandle cases are two examples of situations where the disposition of park land—public land—was more controversial than it was expected to be, and the power of the highway bureaucracies was hotly contested. As we have seen, such conflicts can spread to higher governmental levels, such as the Supreme Court or the Department of Transportation, and gain the support of national environmental groups.

Where park land is not available, freeways are often routed through stabilized neighborhoods. Then displacement of people, businesses, churches, and schools becomes a major source of controversy. Relocation expenses can be high, not only in dollars but also in the unquantifiable emotional costs incurred by those who are displaced. Even those who remain suffer losses. Freeways are not good neighbors. The noise and noxious fumes from heavy traffic generally reduce the value of real estate adjacent to freeways.

While less controversial than freeway construction, the problems of airport development do not have easy solutions either. Their less-controversial nature does not stem from the characteristics of an airport. Air travel seems to be as obnoxious as any other type of transportation: airplanes are noisy, and access roads and parking lots are congested. Airports are less controversial than freeways only because the areas that they affect are concentrated and localized, discouraging large-scale community reaction.

The controversies over heavy rail transit projects are less intense than those over freeways and airports. Railways require smaller areas of right-of-way and they therefore are relatively free of controversy. Their immense cost does, however, cause conflict among governmental entities.

Establishing a bus system excites the least citizen indignation. Buses utilize existing freeway and city-street rights-of-way and therefore require almost no new land acquisition.

As a result of the conflicts over mass transportation, citizens have gained new awareness of how the decisions made by highway bureaucracies and others affect the environment in which they work and live. More and more citizens realize that simply moving out of the path of a new freeway is irresponsible. Instead of avoiding controversies over mass transportation, they must face them head on and solve the difficulties.

One difficulty present in all controversies over urban mass transportation has been the unresponsiveness of the bureaucracy to suggestions made by citizens. It is no wonder bureaucracies feel they are answerable to their superiors, not to the citizenry. Government agencies and their employees have a vital interest in continuing to do what they were created to do. A highway department, for example, staffed by engineers who wish to continue being engineers—planning, constructing, and maintaining highways—will likely be unresponsive to the idea of reducing the number of highways. The result is that important decisions are being made by nonelected officials, and citizens are apt to be underrepresented in the planning, construction, and operation of public mass transit systems.

Critics often point to the slowness in responding to changing social values of the bureaucratic mentality as the source of our continuing difficulties. But it is an inability to cope with changing values, rather than a desire to impede change, that seems to be built into governmental bureaucracies. Because of legislative restrictions and regulations they are inflexible from creation.

All this leads to the larger question. Are science and technology still being employed without paying sufficient attention to the human aspects of changes they bring about? This has become a trite question in many circles. I ask it here to remind the reader that underlying the subject we have undertaken are vast, fundamental questions which I have not attempted to answer.

Controversy over mass transit may arise as a result of the long period from planning stage to operation. The affect of protracted implementation of a plan is that policymakers tend to underrate those changes in social values which may occur during the, say, fifteen years it takes to plan and complete a system like BART. The situation may be somewhat analogous to the planning and building of the Maginot Line, which took over twenty years to complete. By the time it was completed, the manner of warfare had changed completely. The planners had not taken that possibility into account, so much of the effort was wasted. The idea that future social values might be predicted is a fascinating one, but we have little notion, so far, how such foresight might be acquired.

Turning our attention to planning for the present, we face a number of urgent questions. Are urban mass transit planners doing all they can with available techniques to resolve those conflicts that arise between doing a job, completing it as quickly as possible at minimum cost, and performing their moral and social obligations to all citizens potentially affected? Is enough attention paid to considerations that are nonquantifiable, to those aspects of the jobs which cannot be easily reduced to dollars and cents? Who is qualified to handle such matters?

Architects sometimes claim the honor of directing large projects, arguing that they are best qualified because their educations comprise not only technical but aesthetic subjects as well. We may or may not regard their claim as just, depending on what sorts of architectural performances we view around us. But the truth is that the nonquantifiable, nonmonetary, and recalcitrant difficulties have been handled not by architects but by the courts. It appears that the courts have become the only recourse for redress of grievances in public controversial cases. The ordinary citizen has discovered that the parade from office to office in agency headquarters is too often a useless journey. Courts have become the dispensers, and sometimes initiators, of social justice. Legislative branches have enacted laws in response to court decisions. But the question remains: Are the courts the most effective means of dealing with controversy over transportation projects?

It might seem preferable to establish citizen committees to work with and oversee the bureaucracy. Consider the example of Seattle's Transit Advisory Committee, the appointed body which was able to operate successfully in conjunction with the existing bureaucracy to plan transportation investments in that city. One may wonder whether an appointed body can represent citizen interests fairly at all times and in all places. An appointed committee could in itself become bureaucratic, a political plum handed out to sycophants. The experience of many agencies of government illustrates the point. Elected commissions may evade this pitfall.

The public needs to be informed about possible alternative solutions to mass transportation problems. Because decision-making is a process of selection among many alternatives, some of which will not be feasible, it will remain the planner's job to identify all the feasible alternatives.

Although it may seem an obvious point, I believe that the academic background of the decision-maker is vital. University education either early in life or at midpoint is necessary in his professional career. Questions about curriculum requirements occupy university departments continually, but not as frequently in the case of planners, who are generalists, as in the case of students majoring in specific disciplines like chemical engineering or European history. Urban planning requires something like a new kind of Rhodes scholar, someone with intelligence, broadness of technical and humanitarian background, and leadership ability, someone who can competently take responsibility for important and far-reaching decisions.

In *The Octopus*, the dispute between the wheat farmers and the railroad was resolved by gunfire. (The farmers lost the fight.) We have seen who resolves disputes over urban mass transport systems: the courts. And we have seen in whose favor they are resolved: sometimes the bureaucracy, sometimes the people. But court dispute is not such a far cry from the little gun battle 100 years ago in a California valley.

The indignation, the sense of frustration, and the injustice to the injured are just as strong now as they were then. Only the author of that indignation has changed.

"What must we do?" is the question. To answer it, we must ask ourselves another question. "What is wrong with urban mass transit today?"

Most of it is surpassingly ugly. Once the MoPac Freeway in Austin, Texas, was a self-respecting railroad with a right-of-way of 30 or 40 feet. Day after day the trains went by, as they had done for as long as those who lived within the sound of their passage could remember. No one said the Missouri Pacific tracks were beautiful, but people accepted them and considered them necessary. Besides, the houses all along the right-of-way had been built in full recognition of the daily trains. The trains still go by today—in the median of the freeway. You can hardly hear them for the thousands of cars and trucks traveling on the freeway. The continuous growl of engines and wheels can be heard a mile away. The glare of light from passing vehicles and overabundant, badly designed street lamps can be seen for many miles. The right-of-way is now 200 feet wide and the concrete runs like a slash through a deteriorating neighborhood. Yes, it is ugly, as ugly as the trespass against society that brought it into existence.

To create ugliness, noise, and glare is surely a social sin, especially when little good is gained. For who has benefited from the MoPac Freeway? Real-estate developers who have long known that land values rest on accessibility, hauling companies, the construction companies who built it, the highway

department who planned it, and those users who think only of the fifteen minutes it saves them in driving time and close their eyes to the dreariness of
driving it.

And who has lost? Those who live near the freeway, those whose taxes
went to build it, the citizens who will suffer the urban sprawl it is sure to produce, and the city of Austin itself, since it will no longer be quite the pleasant
place to live in that it once was.

But what is "a pleasant place to live in"? It must at least be easy to get
around in: it is not pleasant to spend much time and gasoline to go shopping
or visit the dentist.

Albuquerque is a difficult place to get around in. Imagine the downtown
Albuquerque of forty years ago as a square of rubber. Everything within that
area was relatively easy to reach because of the geometry of a square. Now,
imagine that square of rubber stretching until it became a long, narrow rectangle
something like a rubber band. It is easy to see how inaccessible the places along
the strip have become. The longest distance in one direction one can travel in
the square is its diagonal. The rectangle I have described is like Albuquerque
today. Its diagonal is very close to being the length of its longest side, twenty
or thirty times the diagonal of the original square.

We can forgive those in the past who failed to control such reckless development because they were not aware of the destructive aspects of automobile use.
But what shall we say of those who continue to ruin our towns in this manner,
making transport so inefficient and ugly? At best, they are ignorant; at worst,
venal.

We are back to the original question—"What must we do?" Another
volume—or five or ten—could be written to address that question in detail. But
a brief answer is possible. We must use transport to control our cities, but use
it in full recognition of its many side effects or externalities. For example, in
large cities like New York, there is little reason to allow streets to be congested
and air to be polluted by private cars. Therefore, bar cars from the central
business district. It would represent so forthright an act of manifest good for
the majority of people that all the arguments against the innovation would
seem ephemeral. Public vehicles only in the central business district would be
the rule.

Electrification must be another answer. All heavy rail urban systems are
electrified. Buses should be next. Trolley buses, in use for many years, have
ugly poles and overhead wires and are expensive; even so they are preferable to
high-emission diesel buses. Battery-powered buses may well be perfected before
long, and when they are we should choose them in preference to trolleys and
diesel-fueled vehicles.

And how will you prevent the "Albuquerque effect"? It could not occur
in large cities—or in small ones, either—if transport use were controlled throughout

the whole metropolitan area. We must watch out for parking lots and freeways anywhere in the urban area. In other words, we must beware of the automobile as a mass transit vehicle. It is not suited to the task.

Although it has not been treated specifically in this book, it is obvious that the petroleum price rise of 1973 raised the price of gasoline, and therefore the cost of car use. The cost of urban transportation, which depends to heavily on the automobile, as we have seen in these pages, rose. Future petroleum price rises will have similar effects, but they may put far more strain on car use than we have yet seen. Imagine a price for regular grade of $1.20 per gallon, or even higher. This would cause many more people, especially the poor, to turn to public transit—which will not be there unless we provide it now. This alone, apart from all the other trenchant reasons discussed in this book, is reason enough for moving rapidly to heavy rail, bus, and trolley systems—to traditional mass transit.

The fact is that the United States holds sway over only 50 percent of the petroleum we consume. Thus no control exists over half of the most important resource we use to operate our transport infrastructure. This puts a great part of urban transport partially out of our hands under present arrangements—no price controls and no rationing. A sudden rise in gasoline prices could force the abandonment of the automobile as a mass transit vehicle, with no replacement for it available on short notice. We cannot afford such dependence on the automobile.

Index

Index

About the Author

Henry Malcolm Steiner is a professor of engineering administration at the School of Engineering and Applied Science, The George Washington University, Washington, D.C. He received the bachelor's, master's, and doctoral degrees from Stanford University. Urban transportation and transportation in general have been abiding interests. He has published many articles, numerous reports, and a book of readings in this field. A practicing engineer and economic consultant, he has taught at Mexico City College, ESAN in Lima, Peru, Stanford University, and the University of Texas at Austin.

088131